John Winthrop's Decision for America: 1629

Darrett B. Rutman

University of New Hampshire

The America's Alternatives Series

Edited by **Harold M. Hyman**

John Winthrop's Decision for America: 1629

J.B. Lippincott Company
Philadelphia / New York / Toronto

ISBN 0-397-47332-X
Library of Congress Catalog Card Number 74-31230
Printed in the United States of America

1 3 5 7 9 8 6 4 2

Library of Congress Cataloging in Publication Data

Rutman, Darrett Bruce.
    John Winthrop's decision for America, 1629.

    (The America's alternatives series)
    Bibliography: p.
    1. Winthrop, John, 1588-1649. I. Title.
F67.W7993   974.4'02'0924 [B]   74-31230
ISBN 0-397-47332-X

Contents

Foreword vii
Preface ix
A Note to the Reader xi

PART ONE   Decision for America   1

1   Departure from Yarmouth   3

2   Winthrop's Three Englands   5
The Country   6   The City   7   The Church   8

3   Country Man   13
*"Grevances Groaning for Reformation"   15   The
Court-Country Conflict   17   Winthrop's Place in the
Conflict   18*

4   Calamities   22
The Rise of Arminianism   22   Personal Calamity   24

5   Places to Hide   29
Early Visions of America   31

6   Decision   35
The Final Commitment   36

7   Rationalization   40
Responses to Critics   42

8   Governor Winthrop   45
Preparations for Departure   47

9   In New England   50

PART TWO   Documents of the Decision   53
1   The Social Order   56
2   The Puritan Preacher and the Doctrine of Calling   57
3   The Puritan and the World   61
4   "Common Grevances Groaninge for Reformation"   65
5   Correspondence, 1624-1629   74
6   On "The Lawfulness of Removing out of England"   82
7   "Generall Considerations for the Plantation"   87
8   "Perticular Considerations in the Case of J:W:"   90
9   Winthrop's Answer to a Critic   91
10   "A Modell of Christian Charity"   94

PART THREE   Bibliographic Essay   103

Foreword

"When you judge decisions, you have to judge them in the light of what there was available to do it," noted Secretary of State George C. Marshall to the Senate Committees on the Armed Services and Foreign Relations in May 1951.[1] In this spirit, each volume in the "America's Alternatives" series examines the past for insights which History—perhaps only History—is peculiarly fitted to offer. In each volume the author seeks to learn why decision-makers in crucial public policy or, more rarely, private choice situations adopted a course and rejected others. Within this context of choices, the author may ask what influence then-existing expert opinion, administrative structures, and budgetary factors exerted in shaping decisions? What weights did constitutions or traditions have? What did men hope for or fear? On what information did they base their decisions? Once a decision was made, how was the decision-maker able to enforce it? What attitudes prevailed toward nationality, race, religion, or sex, and how did these attitudes modify results?

We freely ask such questions of the events of our time. This "America's Alternatives" volume transfers appropriate versions of such queries to the past.

In examining those elements that were a part of a crucial historical decision, the author has refrained from making judgments based upon attitudes, information, or values that were not current at the time the decision was made. Instead, as much as possible he or she has explored the past in terms of data and prejudices known to persons contemporary to the event.

1. U.S. Senate, Hearings Before the Committees on the Armed Services and the Foreign Relations to the United States, *The Military Situation in the Far East* (82 Cong., 2d sess.), Part I, p. 382. Professor Ernest R. May's "Alternatives" volume directed me to this source and quotation.

Nevertheless, the following reconstruction of one of America's major alternative choices speaks implicitly and frequently, explicitly to present concerns.

In form, this volume consists of a narrative and analytical historical essay (Part One), within which the author has identified the choice or choices which he believes were actually before the decision makers with whom he is concerned.

Part Two of this volume contains, in whole or part, the most appropriate source documents that illustrate Part One. In turn, Part One will contain references to appropriate Part Two Documents. The volume's Part Three offers users further guidance in the form of a Bibliographic Essay.

It has been and is a self-evident truth to Americans that since the early seventeenth century their fair land has attracted Europeans and Englishmen. Relatively little scholarly attention has gone to the struggles many individuals experienced in the Old World over the question of emigrating or remaining in familiar home contexts. Among the men and women who became British America's first permanent settlers, this option mixed private aspirations, public policies, and divine commandments.

Persons such as John Winthrop discerned the alternatives by means of weighing complex, frequently contradictory, and always troubling factors involved in a decision to relocate in the New World. His decision offers striking insight into the attractions and repulsions that finally nourished a great transatlantic migration. Winthrop's lonely decision was to become part of a great process.

As its heirs, we owe it the respect of understanding its origins. Professor Rutman makes understanding stimulating and accessible.

Harold M. Hyman
Rice University

Preface

History in the past few years has tended more and more to "scientism" and abstraction. If this is a sin, I cheerfully plead guilty for I firmly believe that in the last analysis our understanding of the past is directly related to the degree to which (and the way in which) we merge the abstractions of sociology, psychology, anthropology and the like with historical evidence. Yet the anguished complaint of one student as I wended my way through the complexities of a particular problem of early American social history still rings in my ears: "Where have all the people gone?"

The complaint struck me as ironic on at least four grounds. First, there was the implicit notion that flesh and blood people had been firmly entrenched in the history books up to the point of what some are calling "the new history." (An additional irony: All history is new.) The truth is that historians have habitually subsumed people in generalizations. Second, the basic problem to which historians like myself address ourselves is the relationship of individuals—people—to their society. Third, the great mass of any historian's evidence—the remnant bits and pieces of letters, diaries, journals—is the product of individuals. And finally, history is innately a story-teller's art, and stories are best told when they revolve around people. Momentarily I had forgotten this last, hence engendered my student's complaint. This volume is in one sense a penance.

Its subject is a man—John Winthrop—and his decision to leave the land of his birth and remove to another. Obviously such a decision was not unique to Winthrop. The same decision was made by a good many people in a good many lands and in many different time periods, including, of course, the forebears of every native-born American with the possible exception of the pureblood Indian. Obviously, too, the particulars of this decision will vary from person to person, from time to time. Winthrop was a seventeenth-century English Puritan, whatever that might mean with regard to his decision—and I am not giving away much of the story by saying that I believe it meant a great deal. An emigrant from Slovakia in the late nineteenth century surely cannot be described in the same way. But behind the decision of each lay a subtle interaction of "pushes" and "pulls." There was something in the way the individual discerned his situation in his home society that was pushing him out, and something in his image of another area pulling him in. At the same time, however, there was something in his discernment pulling him to stay and pushing him away—repelling him—from going. The cases of Winthrop, our Slovak emigrant, and all could be studied together and in the abstract, using the language of the psychology of decision making and alienation. Or the abstractions can be used to guide the telling of one unique story.

The latter is the case here. In Part One I have attempted to recreate in narrative form the images of England and America which were in Winthrop's mind, to see the subtle interplay of pushes and pulls which led him to decide the way he did. Except in biography historians seldom work at this level of personal decision-making—as has been said, they prefer to generalize from the actions of many people—hence the body of prior interpretation is scant. But in footnotes to Part One and in an appended brief note this aspect of the subject is made available to the reader. Narrative, notes, and (above all) the inclusion in Part Two of most of the relevant documents opens for the student the whole process of creative history—the merger of question, method, prior interpretation, and documentation which underlies any historian's story.

A number of people greatly facilitated the preparation of the volume. The enthusiasm of the series editor, Harold M. Hyman, when the subject was first broached to him encouraged the attempt. And, of course, the volume would have been impossible without the cooperation of the Massachusetts Historical Society which owns the great bulk of the pertinent documents, and the direct assistance of John D. Cushing and Malcolm Freiberg of the Society's staff.

Darrett B. Rutman
The University of New Hampshire

Note to Reader ═══════════════════════

Some of the language in the quotations of Part One and the documents section, Part Two of this volume, is archaic or at least unfamiliar to the modern reader. The meanings of particular terms are easily obtained in the *Oxford English Dictionary*, but for the most part can be inferred from the context of the documents themselves. The only source of confusion to be cleared up for the reader is the usage of the abbreviation *li.* for the English pound sterling.

Part One

Decision for America

1

Departure from Yarmouth

On Thursday, April 8, 1630, John Winthrop left his homeland, sailing from Yarmouth on England's Isle of Wight aboard the *Arbella* bound for America and New England.[1] With him were his sons Stephen and Adam, ages ten and nine respectively; a third son, Henry, twenty-one years old, was to have sailed with them, but Henry quite literally missed the boat. Behind in England Winthrop left his wife Margaret, eight months pregnant, and five other children: Samuel, just over two; Deane, age six; Mary, seventeen; a son Forth, twenty; and his eldest son, John Junior, twenty-three, whose charge it was to sell the family land and, once Winthrop was firmly settled, bring Margaret and the others to America. Margaret's rejoining him, however, was in the future; for now, to John, sailing meant agonized separation. Five days before, while the *Arbella* lay waiting for a favorable wind, he had written one last letter of goodbye.

> O, how loth am I to bidd thee Farewell, but since it must be, Farewell, my sweet love, farewell: Farewell my deare children and familye, the Lord bless you all, and grant me to see your faces once againe. come (my deare) take him and let him rest in thine armes, who will ever remaine Thy faithfull husband.[2]

Over the centuries individual Europeans in their thousands would undertake a voyage similar to Winthrop's. In one sense, Winthrop stands out. He was the leader of a major colonizing venture. Aboard the *Arbella* and ten other ships of what is known as "the Winthrop fleet" were one thousand settlers, the largest single exodus of Englishmen going to America to date. Sailing to an area of the American coast boasting at the moment only a handful of Englishmen, Winthrop and his company would establish the colony of Massachusetts Bay and by their initial success attract ten thousand additional emigrants over the next few years, making Massachusetts one of the largest and most prosperous of England's overseas outposts. His departure was, therefore, a public as well as a private act, with public as well as private consequences.

Yet in another sense, Winthrop was one with all the others who left Europe for America, the great and small. At some point prior to the actual sailing he—as any other—had to make a private decision to abandon the relative security of established ways for the relative insecurity of something new, to give up all he had and truly knew for something he could only imagine, to hazard a dangerous journey and divide his family without real assurance that the family would ever be together again. For each individual this private decision was awesome. The sum of such decisions peopled America.

Winthrop's departure from Yarmouth was, of course, after the fact of the decision. Yarmouth, therefore, is the culmination rather than the beginning of our story. The decision itself was made probably in early August of 1629, specifically at Tattershall, the home of the Earl of Lincoln. Yet the decision, too, was a culmination. Winthrop was, through a lengthy portion of his life, increasingly dissatisfied in England—alienated is our modern word. At some point he became aware of a potential in New England for a fulfillment which he felt was denied him in old England. Alienation and the awareness of a New England potential ultimately worked together, the first pushing him from the kingdom, the second pulling him to New England, until all that held him in England was overcome and the decision for America became, in his mind, an imperative: "How loth am I to bidd thee Farewell," he wrote Margaret from the *Arbella*, "but since *it must be*, Farewell." Our task is to understand the dynamics by which this imperative developed.

Notes

1. During the period dates were written according to the Julian calendar and the new year began in March. The Julian dates have been retained here but the year dates have been adjusted to make January 1 the New Year's day. To transpose the dates to the modern Gregorian calendar add 10 days.

2. Winthrop to Margaret Winthrop, April 3, 1630, Massachusetts Historical Society, *Winthrop Papers* (Boston, 1929-47), vol. II, p. 229.

2

Winthrop's Three Englands

From birth to manhood is a process of ever expanding one's horizons, although in the premodern world of the late sixteenth and early seventeenth centuries the ultimate limit of those horizons was largely dictated by the station of life into which one was born. A gentleman's son would ultimately see and sense more of the world than the son of a poor farmer. John Winthrop was a gentleman's son, born in 1588—the year of the Spanish Armada—to a family newly risen to the rank of landed gentry.[1] His grandfather, Adam (1498-1562), had laid the basis of the family's position by amassing money as a London cloth merchant and buying Groton Manor in County Suffolk, fifty-odd miles northeast of the city; his father, again Adam (1548-1623), the sixth of old Adam's sons and a lawyer, came to own Groton a few years after John's birth. Groton manor house, its rolling fields, and the schooling given him by a nearby minister were undoubtedly among John's earliest memories. Yet his horizons grew rapidly. At fifteen he was off to Trinity College, Cambridge. At seventeen his father contracted a marriage for him, with Mary Forth of a landed Essex County family, a marriage which brought him land, fatherhood—John Winthrop, Jr. was born at Groton in 1606 when John was but eighteen—and what presumably was his first significant exposure to religion. John himself wrote much later of this last:

> About 18 years of age (being a man in stature, and in understanding as my parents conceived mee) I married into a family under Mr. Culverwell his ministry in Essex; and living there sometimes I first found the ministry of the word to come to my heart with power (for in all before I found onely light) and after that I found the like in the ministry of many others. So as there began to bee some change which I perceived in my self, and others took notice of. Now I began to come under strong exercises of Conscience: . . . I could no longer dally with Religion.[2]

John's horizons were still expanding. In 1613 his father entered him in Gray's Inn in London to begin reading in the law. John would follow his father's profession, eventually developing a London law practice which would force him to divide his time between the city and his country lands. In 1615 the marriage of his youth ended with the death of Mary Forth, leaving John (now twenty-six) a widower with four children; a second marriage ended tragically within a year, and in 1618, after briefly courting Margaret Tyndal, the daughter of another Essex landed family, he married a third time. By then, however, he had taken over the management of Groton from his father. A few years later father Adam died. "He hathe finished his course," John,

5

now the head of the family, wrote; he "is gathered to his people in peace, as the ripe corne into the barne."[3]

The Country

Groton and the life of a country gentlemen was one of three Englands which Winthrop came to know in his rise to maturity. The house itself had disappeared by the mid-nineteenth century—only a cellar hole and a mulberry tree which graced the garden plot remained. But we can envision it as typical to its time: set on some 160 acres overlooking the river Box and about a half-mile from Groton Church and the village, it rose two stories high with a steeply pitched roof affording additional space for a garret. A great hall and parlor shared the first floor with kitchen, buttery, pantry, and dairy; on the second floor were bed chambers for the family, while in the garret were beds for the maid servants, and perhaps for the children as well.[4] Clustering about the house were barns and outbuildings housing crops and equipment, animals and male servants. The whole formed what historian R.H. Tawney has called "a miniature cooperative society," housed together, dependent upon one industry (agriculture) "and including not only man and wife and children, but servants and labourers, ploughmen and threshers, cowherds and milkmaids."[5] The gardens and fields worked from the manor house itself were only one part of Winthrop's holdings, however. Hard by the church was Groton Hall with its 60 acres, perhaps worked by laborers. And scattered through the countryside were farms and cottages worked by tenants. In all there were over 515 acres which Winthrop, in 1629, estimated as providing an income of 430 pounds sterling a year, a good but not great sum for that time. The Winthrops had at least two other extensive holdings as well, one at nearby Lavenham, the other at Stambridge in Essex.

There was a busyness to this country world. The broad acres which John had hunted as a youth (albeit without much success) he now rode over as master. Servants had to be overseen; that they would squander their time and their master's substance was proverbial. Rents and debts had to be collected (and paid), not always an easy task when hard times hit the countryside. There was much coming and going of relatives and friends as well, for the Winthrop circle was large and hospitality a rule. But this country world was most marked by a sense of precedence and deference—precedence, and with it responsibility, being assumed within the family by the father (Adam in John's youth, then by John himself) and by the manor family within the village community; deference being accorded by wife, children, and servants to the father and by the many families of the community toward the gentry family of the manor.

Precedence, deference, and responsibility were part of the fabric of John's country life. As a child he undoubtedly sat quietly in the background as father Adam marked the day's end with a lengthy reading from the Bible; John, as father, took his place at the head of the great table in Groton's hall to read the Bible aloud to his own family. Just as father Adam had taken

John up to Cambridge to place him in college, then settled him on the land and in the profession of law, so John directed the education of his own children. Having sent John Jr. to Trinity College, Dublin, in the early 1620s (subsequently he would place him in London to read law), John wrote him that "there is nothinge in this world that can be like cause of private comfort to me as to see the wellfare of my children. . . . think not of seeinge England till you may bringe a hood at your backe."[6] Similarly, John as a child might well have watched as his father held forth among the villagers assembled in the manor court, dealing with their petty offenses and resolving disputes and trespasses; but his majority was marked in 1609 by his father's allowing *him* to hold court. There was a quiet immemorialness to this progression from father to son, a sense of an unchanging past and present that both reflected and was bolstered by a traditional view of society which Winthrop imbibed as a boy from his family, his teachers, the ministers of his church, and which ruled him as a man. God, this view held, in one instant, had "created & appointed all thinges in heaven, earth, & waters, in a most excellente & perfecte order;" similarly, He created men and women in their "degree . . . vocation, callyng & office." Given such a view, one's obligations were simple: to labor "in that state of life unto which it shall please God to call me"—so read the catechism of the church; to submit "lowly and reverently to all my betters" while caring for all my inferiors; to eschew ambition and personal gain in the interest of the ordered community (Document 1).[7]

The City

The practice of law carried Winthrop away from his country world and into a second England sharply contrasting with the first. Much of his work, in common with that of any country lawyer, was the dull routine of conveyances and marriage settlements. But the law set him riding the road to Bury St. Edmunds where the court of quarter sessions for John's part of the county met. As he traveled and in the courts he could not but be aware of at least the symptoms of a changing, restless England undergoing complex social and economic adjustments: an abundance of poverty, embracing both the settled poor of the villages and ranging vagabonds of the roads; idleness in some, surging acquisitiveness in others; drunkenness and moral laxity; inflation and a population which, to some observers, seemed to be growing at a rate faster than the society could absorb. "The People," wrote a commentator of 1609, "doe swarme in the land, as young bees in a hive in June; insomuch that there is very hardly roome for one man to live by another. The mightier like old strong bees thrust the weeker, as younger, out of their hives."[8] And increasingly Winthrop's law work sent him to raucous, jangling London, the very antithesis of quiet Groton.

In London the relatively single-minded pursuit of agriculture of Groton gave way to a kaleidoscope of occupations, the familial unity of the manor and village to avaricious competitiveness. "In London," a critic of the city wrote, "the ritch disdayne the poor. The Courtier the Cittizen. The Cittizen the Countriman. One Occupation disdayneth another. The Merchant the Retayler. The Retayler the Craftsman. The better sort of Craftsman the baser. The Shoomaker the Cobbler. The Cobbler the Carman."[9] In London, too, the relatively simple sins of the villagers seemed to give way to the most perfidious; a whole section of the city—unsafe for the innocent after dark—was given over to bear pits and theaters, puppet shows and brothels; the very porch of St. Paul's Cathedral was the hunting ground of cutpurses. Above all, London, together with nearby Westminster—the seat of king and parliament—was an arena of politics alien to country Groton.

Winthrop during his adult life lived under two monarchs, James I, who came to the throne at the death of Elizabeth in 1603 and died in the spring of 1625, and James's son Charles. For Winthrop, James and Charles were more than the symbols of sovereignty and loyalty that the English monarch is today, although they were that, of course. They were, in brief, personal governors; the care of the kingdom was the king's responsibility, shared in part with a handful of privy councillors and great lords of state whom he appointed (and rewarded), and by them with their proteges to whom they granted (or, more often, sold) lesser offices. So, too, was the care of the English Protestant church the responsibility of the king (shared with a royally appointed hierarchy of bishops and archbishops), the administration of justice (shared with the king's judges), and the conduct of foreign affairs. The way of this structure was implicit, and about the person of the king clustered the courtiers (with their ladies), some as officeholders with a share in governing, others merely aspiring for a share, all sharing in the pleasures of an ostentatious, sensuous, and, to such as Winthrop, scandalous court life.[10]

Such personal government was an expensive proposition, particularly for kings who persisted in enriching their favorites or who were rash enough to commit expensive arms and men to overseas wars. The monarch's personal and customary revenues all too frequently came up short, even when, in novel ways, they tried to expand the latter, and kings appealed to the generosity of the nation by summoning a parliament of noble peers and the hierarchy of the church (the House of Lords), and of elected gentlemen (the House of Commons). More likely than not, however, the Parliament so summoned, particularly the Commons, would attempt to withhold its generosity in an attempt to bring the king to act in ways it felt most proper, setting the stage for angry, wrangling sessions over such issues as the royal favorites, monopolies granted by the monarch to individual courtiers, the king's prerogative and his novel exactions. The Parliament of 1614 was an example; James had ended it after a fruitless two months, imprisoning three of the members of the Commons for intemperate and seditious speeches.

The Church

Winthrop's third England was that of Puritanism. There is no need here to retell the involved story of the English Reformation and the rise of

Puritanism.[11] Suffice it to say that the nub of the Puritan movement was an ardent, evangelical preaching ministry. Ezekiel Culverwell—who had awakened Winthrop to a concern for religion—was one such minister; so too were William Perkins, Richard Rogers, and Robert Bolton whose books we know Winthrop subsequently read. A self-conscious minority within the English clergy, they brushed aside forms and ceremonies which tended to make religion easy for men and preached a blunt (and to us hard) doctrine: men must realize that they were merely God's dependent creatures—servants—and must be ever about God's work. God would have them honor and obey His moral law—but far more! God gave men their places and their work in this world, and they must do it humbly, quietly, for His sake, not their own. God placed pleasures in the world, and again men must undertake to relish these pleasures, but for His sake and not for the sake of the pleasures themselves. God placed sin in the world and commanded men to avoid it, but it was part of God's plan that they could *not* live free of sin. Above all, God made life transitory; for His sake they must accept death—indeed, it was release from the inevitability of sin—and the subsequent glorification or damnation which, for His own unfathomable purposes, God had planned for each man individually (Document 2).

In all of this, Puritanism was intensely personal—a matter of conscience—and evoked a personal response.[12] In Winthrop it exaggerated that sense of one's duty to labor in a God-ordained calling already remarked by underscoring the immediacy of God to the individual. God, so to speak, was ever at his shoulder, directing him to the things at which he must labor. True, there was a difficulty in differentiating between the promptings of God and those of sinful ego. In the immediate aftermath of his awakening by Culverwell, for example, Winthrop thought himself duty-bound to serve as a preacher himself, but introspection (and the advice of friends) led him to see it was a false call. There was "much hollownes and vaine glory" in his heart, and he found his duty to lie not in public preaching but in ministering to his family, writing "that the conscionable and constant teachinge of my familye was a speciall businesse, wherein I might please God, and greatly further their and mine owne salvation."[13] (To one of his letters to her, Winthrop's wife Margaret once responded: "I hope through Gods blessinge your paynes will not be all together lost. . . . those serious thoughts of your owne which you sent me did make a very good supply in stead of a sarmon.")[14] But whenever Winthrop determined that a call to labor came from God he attacked the work with vehemence. Thus when elevated to the local judiciary as a justice of the peace, he conceived of his elevation in godly terms and his duties to be godly duties; when he sensed that he was not ardent enough in his performance of those duties he felt that he was failing God and wrote bitterly against himself for his "remissnesse in my callinge of magistracie, in that I had not been painfull in the findinge out and zealous in the punishinge of sinne."[15] Presumably he reformed, to the chagrin of the idlers, drunkards, and harlots with whom he dealt.

Yet Winthrop's conviction of the godliness of a call could lapse in a moment. Vehemence in his labor brought him wordly rewards, both financial and an all-too-human sense of satisfaction. He mulled over his "secret sinnes and corruptions" and prayed agonizingly that God would bolster and support his human frailty. He torturously examined his way (was he God's proper servant or not?), alternately relished his work and its rewards, then abandoned both when he sensed that because he relished them so much the work itself was not God's but his. The inner conflict is a key to much of Winthrop's character. For indeed he *was* ambitious for worldly things, but, God-heavy, he regularly frustrated ambition. In a diary of his religious "Experiencia" which he sporadically kept, he put this ambition and frustration well. All about him, he wrote at one time, men lauded "wisdome, glorye, wealthe, pleasure," while he took comfort only in thoughts of heavenly things. Was he a fool "to sett so light by honour, credite, welthe, jollitie? . . . Methought I hearde all men telling me I was" (Document 3).

O Lord keepe me that I be not discouraged, neither thinke the more meanly of the portion which I have chosen, even to walke with thee.[16]

Puritanism imparted still more to Winthrop. As the most dynamic aspect of the Protestant Reformation in England, Puritanism exaggerated in Winthrop a pervasive English suspicion and hostility toward Rome and Catholicism. Rising coincidentally with a rising tide of English nationalism, Puritanism commingled with nationalism. Winthrop's England was Shakespeare's England as well, and it was Shakespeare who wrote of

.... this scepter'd isle, ...
This blessed plot, this earth, this realm,
this England.

"God," John Aylmer wrote, "is English"; England, Winthrop echoed, must come closer to God's way than any other nation, for it is God's favorite.[17] Emanating from the preachers, Winthrop's Puritanism tied him to the cause of the preachers as they sought to reform the English church, to make it simply a pulpit from which God's preachers preached, to rid it of those many clerics content to mumble a service now and again and enjoy the good life of the priesthood between times. And because he was so attuned to the preachers, Winthrop's Puritanism set as the background for his adult life a veritable cacaphony of lamentations and Jeremiah-like prophecies of imminent doom and desolation. For the preachers were bitterly critical of England. God was not honored as they would have him honored, and they held up Sabbath breaking as a cardinal sin. They tended to transform traditional values—those that Winthrop had imbibed at Groton—into God-ordained ordinances and castigate the falling away from those values as sin. Except for the vehemence of their expression, there was nothing really new in the social message of the preachers, in their condemnation of covetousness, for example:

He abuseth his calling, whosoever he be that against the end thereof, imploves it for himselfe, seeking wholly his own, & not the common good. And that common saying, *Every man for himself, and God for us all,* is wicked, and is directly against the end of every calling or honest kinde of life (Document 2).[18]

When England would not reform its ways—indeed, in the preachers' eyes, they grew worse through the 1620s as the English church hierarchy seemingly turned toward Catholicism (a phenomenon we shall take note of)—the preachers could only threaten divine judgment.

> What hath God found in England? . . . He looks for obedience but beholds rebellion, contempt. He looks that we should be brought to a right frame by all our blessings, his pains, his judgments. He looks we should wait on God and come nearer to him. . . . But we grow worse and dishonor Him.
> God is going, his glory is departing, England hath seen her best days, and now evil days are befalling us: God is packing up his Gospel, because no body will buy his wares, nor come to his price.[19]

Notes

1. There is no major modern biography of Winthrop. Robert C. Winthrop, *Life and Letters of John Winthrop* (Boston: Ticknor and Fields, 1863-66) is largely a filiopiestic printing of Winthrop letters but gives the broad outlines of Winthrop's life; Joseph Hopkins Twichell, *John Winthrop* (New York: Dodd, Mead, and Co., 1891) adds little. Edmund S. Morgan, *The Puritan Dilemma: The Story of John Winthrop* (Boston: Little, Brown, 1958) is short but highly suggestive, as is Part III of Samuel Eliot Morison's *Builders of the Bay Colony* (Boston and New York, 1930) and the first part of Richard S. Dunn's *Puritans and Yankees: The Winthrop Dynasty of New England, 1630-1717* (Princeton, N.J.: Princeton University Press, 1962). John Winthrop Jr. is reasonably well served by Robert C. Black, III, *The Younger John Winthrop* (New York: Comumbia University Press, 1966); Margaret Winthrop less so in Alice Morse Earle's *Margaret Winthrop* (New York: C. Scribner's Sons, 1895).

2. Winthrop, "Christian Experience," Mass. Hist. Soc., *Winthrop Papers*, vol. I, p. 155.

3. Winthrop to John Winthrop, Jr., June 26, 1623, ibid., p. 282.

4. Chapter 10 of H.P.R. Finberg, ed., *The Agrarian History of England and Wales*, (Cambridge: At the University Press, 1967), vol. 4, *1500-1640*, ed. Joan Thirsk, is suggestive on "rural housing in England."

5. In *The Agrarian Problem in the Sixteenth Century* (London: Longmans, Green and Co., 1912), p. 233.

6. Letter of October 3, 1623, Mass. Hist. Soc., *Winthrop Papers*, vol. I, p. 289-90.

7. From "An Exhortation, concernynge good order & obedience, to rulers and Majestrates" in *Certayne Sermons appoynted by the Queenes Majestie, to be declared and read* (London, 1562), no pagination. [*See Part 2, Document 1.*] The catechism of the Church of England (composed in 1549 and still in use) is quoted from Peter Laslett, *The World we have lost* (New York: Scribner, 1965), p. 176, a provocative introduction to preindustrial England.

8. William Symonds, *Virginia. A Sermon* (London: E. Edgar and W. Welly, 1609), excerpted in, *The Genesis of the United States: A Narrative of the Movement in England, 1605-1616, which Resulted in the Plantation of North America by Englishmen*, ed., Alexander Brown (London: 1890), vol. I, p. 288.

9. Thomas Nashe (1593) quoted in Carl Bridenbaugh, *Vexed and Troubled Englishmen: 1590-1642* (New York: Oxford University Press, 1968), p. 188.

10. For summaries see Wallace Notestein, *The English People on the Eve of Colonization, 1603-1630* (New York: Harper, 1954) and G.P.V. Akrigg, *Jacobean Pageant: or, The Court of King James I* (Cambridge, Mass.: Harvard University Press, 1962).

11. See A.G. Dickens, *The English Reformation* (New York: Schocken Books, 1964); Patrick Collinson, *The Elizabethan Puritan Movement* (Berkeley and Los Angeles: University of California Press, 1967); William Haller, *The Rise of Puritanism* (New York: Columbia University Press, 1938).

12. On the response to Puritanism generally see Darrett B. Rutman, *American Puritanism: Faith and Practice* (Philadelphia: Lippincott, 1970); for the particular case of Winthrop, see Morgan's *Puritan Dilemma*, chap. 1.

13. Winthrop, "Christian Experience" and "Experiencia." Mass. Hist. Soc., *Winthrop Papers*, vol. I, pp. 157, 213. [*For the latter see Part 2, Document 3.*]

14. Letter of ca. May 18, 1629, ibid., vol. II, p. 92.

15. Winthrop, "Experiencia," ibid., vol. I, p. 205.

16. Ibid., pp. 212, 195-96. [*See Part 2, Document 3.*]

17. Shakespeare, *Richard II,* act II, scene i, lines 40, 50; Aylmer (1559) quoted in Peter Gay, *A Loss of Mastery: Puritan Historians in Colonial America* (Berkeley and Los Angeles: University of California Press, 1966), p. 6. See also William Haller, *The Elect Nation* (New York: Columbia University Press, 1963).

18. William Perkins, *A Treatise of the Vocations, or Callings of men, with sorts and kinds of them, and the right use thereof, in The Workes of that Famous and Worthy Minister . . . Mr. William Perkins* (London: I. Legatt, 1612), vol. I, pp. 750-752. [*See Part 2, Document 2.*]

19. Sermon of John Wilson, May 18, 1628, Robert Keayne's MS Journal of English Sermons, 1628, Massachusetts Historical Society, Boston; Thomas Hooker (1630), quoted in David D. Hall, *The Faithful Shepherd: A History of the New England Ministry in the Seventeenth Century* (Chapel Hill: University of North Carolina Press, 1972), p. 77.

3

Country
Man

Groton, London, Puritanism—Winthrop's three Englands—fixed his mind in the mold of a "Country man." The phrase is important, for throughout the early seventeenth century England's gentlemen—the social and political elite of the realm—were dividing into "Court" and "Country," what historian Lawrence Stone has described as two distinct and hostile cultures.[1] The dichotomization was deep. The Court cultivated novelty, the Country tradition. The Court countenanced personal ambition. The Country ennobled the idea of quiet, patriarchal service. The Court, individually, fixed its vision (and ambition) upon the national government of the king. The Country thought in terms of local government, of Parliament as representing propertied constituencies, and of the king as bound by the necessity of the common good and the precedents of a common law. The Court seemed isolated from the everyday problems of the nation. The Country man lived, so to speak, with those problems. The Court was enthralled by London, "the garden of England," one called it, where one found "rich wives, spruce mistresses, pleasant houses, good dyet, rare wines, neat servants, fashionable furniture, pleasures and profits the best of all sorts."[2] The Country man detested the City and magnified country virtues. Stone summarizes succinctly: the Country was "an ideal," a "vision of rustic arcadia."

> It was a vision of environmental superiority over the City: The Country was peaceful and clean, a place of grass and trees and birds, the City was ugly and dirty and noisy, a place of clattering carts and coaches, coal dust and smog, and piles of human excrement. It was also a vision of moral superiority over the Court; the Country was virtuous, the Court wicked; the Country was thrifty, the Court extravagant; the Country was honest; the Court corrupt.[3]

Above all, the Court took religion lightly—even countenancing Catholicism—while the Country was stolidly Protestant and, in such as Winthrop, Puritan. To him, Country values were godly values, the dichotomy between Country and Court equatable to that between good and evil, and the evil of the Court portentous of God's wrath against the nation—that wrath which the Puritan preachers both lamented and promised. And Winthrop could reverse this last to envision social or natural disasters as the exercise of God's wrath brought on by a falling away from godly Country ways.

This was certainly the case in January 1622 when, from Groton, Winthrop wrote to his London brother-in-law, Thomas Fones, expressing his "sense of the present evill tymes, and the feare of worse"; "The Lo: looke mercifully upon this sinfull lande, and turne us to him by some repentance, otherwise we may feare it hath seene the best dayes."[4] In the countryside there were crop failures and depression, in London scandalous ostentation among uncaring courtiers. A popular ballad pointed the contrast:

> . . . poore men still enforced are
> To pay more than they are able.
> Methought I heard them weeping say,
> Their substance was but small;
> For rich men will beare all the sway,
> And poore men pay for all.[5]

In London, too, still another Parliament had met, wrangled with the monarch, and been dissolved. Abroad, the forces of a Catholic Holy Roman Emperor had driven the newly crowned Protestant king of Bohemia—and King James's son-in-law to boot—from his throne; Catholic Spain had joined the emperor and the Catholic forces were harassing the erstwhile king in his native Palatinate. But far from bringing England into the fray on God's side, King James was contemplating an alliance with Spain, sealed by the marriage of his son Charles to a Spanish, Catholic princess.

Into 1623 the times—and Winthrop's mood, as he saw God's wrath in the times—remained bleak. Prince Charles and the current royal favorite, the duke of Buckingham, went off to Spain itself to court the Spanish princess, at a cost of ten thousand English pounds. From Lincolnshire, one county removed from Winthrop's Suffolk, a country gentleman wrote of

> many thousands in these parts who have sold all they have even to their bed-straw, and cannot get work to earn any money. Dog's flesh is a dainty dish, and found upon search in many houses, also such horse flesh as hath lain long in a deke for hounds, and the other day one stole a sheep, who for mere hunger tore a leg out.[6]

From London, just before Christmas in 1623, Winthrop wrote to Margaret at Groton that "provision be made; and all our poore feasted, though I be from home, so I shalbe the lesse missed."[7]

It is during these troubled days of the early 1620s that we discern Winthrop for the first time active in the affairs of the nation—not central to them, but involved, while to this point he had been simply an onlooker, the Country gentleman and lawyer occasionally in London. In September of 1623 Prince Charles and Buckingham returned from Spain, their enthusiasm for the Spanish marriage dampened by their poor reception in Madrid. Now they pressed for a good Protestant war against Spain and the calling of Parliament, joining their Court voices to a Country demand. Winthrop looked forward to the event, staying on in wintry London to be at the center of the great doings. Every rumor he sent home to Groton and Margaret until, on January 1, he gleefully reported the certainty that Parliament would meet in February. As the Parliament opened, with Winthrop not a member but apparently in attendance at its committees, he reported that it was "begunne with exceedinge muche comfort and hope: the treatye about the Spanish matche is now concluded by king prince and Parliament to be at an ende; and it is very like we shall not holde longe with Spain . . . the Duke of Buckingham hathe quitt himself worthely and given great satisfaction to the Parliament. God sende a good ende to these happie beginnings."[8]

Winthrop clearly—as every good Country man in and about this Parliament of 1624—was concerned over the Spanish marriage and the war in Europe. These were the central events of the moment. His concerns relative to affairs at home are equally clear. Even in late November or early December 1623, while the calling of Parliament was still only conjectural, he outlined to Sir Robert Crane (who would serve in the House of Commons from Suffolk) a series of measures to better the affairs of both church and countryside. The letter itself has not survived the vicissitudes of time, but a list of "Common Grevances Groaninge for Reformation" has (Document 4). Presumably the work of several Suffolk County gentlemen, the extant copy is in part in Winthrop's handwriting and can be assumed to contain at least the gist of his suggestions to Sir Robert.[9]

"Grevances Groaning for Reformation"

In religious matters the grievances reflect the vehement anti-Catholicism of the Puritan Country man, the very first grievance cited being "the daylye encrease of the multitudes of papistes" whose "wicked myndes" are "all wayes in study and action howe to betray" England and the king "into the handes of forreigne power [the Pope], the greatest adversary which our Land hath." The remedy proposed: "Some fundamentall lawe . . . to remove all theire Children from them, to be trained up in the truth." The cause of the Puritan preachers—Winthrop's sound, godly preachers—was reflected as well. On the one hand, too many were being suspended, their preaching silenced because of their disregard for the forms and ceremonies insisted upon by the church hierarchy. "These ceremonyes," it was argued, "ar by our ch[urch] of England holden to be but thinges indifferent, and noe parte of godes worshipp." Godly preachers should be allowed to "employ themselves in theire minystery to holsome doctrine and exhortacon" so long as they "live peaceably and quietly in their calling and shall not by writeing or preacheing impugne thinges established." Too many others could not find adequate employment because of the practice of plural benefices—in effect, one man at the same time serving two, three, and more churches. The solution: divide pluralities and let no man hold forth in more than one parish. On the other hand, too many scandalous and nonpreaching ministers—"dombe" ministers in the parlance of the time—were tolerated, men who "doe much harme by their example, murthering many thousand sowles, which is a crying sinne." All such should be removed within six months and their pulpits turned over to "godly Learned and paynefull" preachers. And until every English pulpit was filled by a godly preacher, no man should be barred (as the law currently barred him) from going "to another parrish to heare a sermon when there is none in their owne parrish."

The localism of the Country man and his antipathy toward an overweening and ever-enlarging central authority (be it the authority of the king, his courts, or of the ecclesiastical hierarchy) were displayed in the grievances as well. That indictments brought before local courts were being removed to the king's courts at Westminister was wrong. So, too, was "the multitude of Atturnies in the Courtes at West[minster]" who "upon very slight occasions, and often upon meere suggestions" provoked trivial litigation which profited none but themselves. So, too, was the trial of "adultery, whoredome Inceste and such lyke" before ecclesiastical courts without informing the minister and parish where the offense took place, and the commutation of ecclesiastical punishments into money fines payable to a bishop's treasury rather than to the local parish chest. Royal patents or "briefs" authorizing their bearers to collect money for charitable purposes within the churches were wrong; not only did such collections "much disturbe the devine service and the worshipp of God," but the frequent spuriousness of the briefs and the fact that they called for money in excess of what was needed in order to pay the commissions of the "brief farmers" who actually undertook the collections tended to "cutt the throate of charitie amongst all men." And the evil was compounded. That charity was dead worsened the lot of the poor. The remedy proposed: "That every Conty might releive theire owne poore and yf the towne be not able, that the Justices might take order at the quarter Sessions to releeve them" out of the king's funds or from local taxes.

For the rest, the "Grevances" were a curious melange—"the extraordinary casualties and divastation by fyers," "the decay of the aunciente Trade of Sadlers," "the greate decay of feasants and patriges with an excedinge disorder in haukeinge," "the common scarcitie of woode and tymber." One thing seems to bind this miscellany together: a concern in the mind of the authors of the "Grevances" for a general corrosiveness abroad in the land, eating away at the vitals of a sound society. Fires were the result of the slackness of men and women in the pursuit of their callings, "untrustines of recles servantes, heedeles dames, careles maisters, and a supine negligence in all sorts." Wood was scarce because the owners of woodlots were discouraged from their work "by the unrewlines of the poorer sort, whoe doe from tyme to tyme by day and night make all havoke and wast of any thing that is cherished and preserved." That both saddlers and pheasants were disappearing was due to too many men pretending to too high a station in life. That proper differences between the ranks of society existed—between the nobility and the common gentlemen on the one hand and between the gentlemen and the "meaner sort" on the other—was demonstrable "from the lawe of nature order and antiquitie." (Winthrop in a later writing would add God's edict as a determinant.) "But rather than leave the gentle recreation of hawking to their betters, many of the very meane sort and condicion . . . have presumed of this generous skill" to the effect that "the wonted store of game, which was wont liberally to furnish both prince noble and gentle is now spoyled and destroyed." And rather than ride horseback (as Winthrop invariably did), hence giving work to the saddlers who produced the equipage, overly ambitious gentlemen and their ladies were usurping the carriages and coaches "anciently the furniture . . . and honorable privelidges of Emperors, Kinges, great princes, nobles and other greate worthies."

The "Common Grevances" felt by Winthrop and his fellow Suffolk gentlemen seem to have received short shrift in the Parliament. Sir Robert, upon receiving Winthrop's outline, had predicted as much, even putting Winthrop off, at least in part. Hopefully "God of his mersy," he had responded, would take care of "all thinges that may be hinderanse to his triue worshipe; for the other bisinases, they wilbe acseptable (and no doute profitable) to the common welthe but I beleve it is not that which moveth

[the calling of Parliament] but sum suplye of muny" for the war.[10] He was
not entirely correct, for the Parliament did move to effect some reforms. But
only a few related to the issues raised in the "Grevances." A petition from the
Parliament led to a royal proclamation expelling from England all Jesuits,
seminary priests, and persons in Romish orders; another petition protested
the excess of charitable briefs; and an act of Parliament attempted "to
prevent the abuses" in removing cases from the counties to the royal
courts.[11] Winthrop evidenced no dejection at this poor response, however.
The pessimism of 1622—the "sence of the present evill tymes"—did not
immediately return. Having been moved by that pessimism, it seems that
Winthrop had optimistically involved himself in England's governing system
(albeit on the fringe) and there, for the moment, he remained.

The Court-Country Conflict

Yet Winthrop's optimism, in common with the optimism of every Puritan
and the Country as a whole, was a fragile thing. True, the Country had its
Protestant war in Germany and against Spain; England even blundered into a
civil war in France, coming to the aid of French Protestants and adding the
French monarchy to its list of enemies. But the wars were consistently
underfinanced and badly bungled. Expedition after expedition—to Germany,
to Spanish Cadiz, to French La Rochelle—came straggling back through the
Channel ports, the men defeated, sick, demoralized. In Parliament, the
Country blamed the Court and particularly the Duke of Buckingham: "Our
honour is ruined," one Country leader thundered; "our ships are sunk, our
men perished, not by the sword, not by an enemy, not by chance, but . . . by
those we trust."[12]

True, too, that in March 1625 James I died; the prince, now Charles I, was
essentially of sterner moral fiber than his father, and the way of the Court
changed radically. Crude obscenities which had amused James were no longer
tolerated; neither were the tasteless extravagances of James's time. But
Buckingham remained the royal favorite until his murder in 1628 and, in the
Country mind, the stereotype of the courtier. To the Parliament of 1626
another Country leader would cite Buckingham's "profuse expenses, his
superfluous feasts, his magnificent buildings, his riots, his excesses."[13]
Moreover, although Charles had no Spanish Catholic wife, James, before his
death, had arranged for Charles's marriage to a French—and Catholic—
princess, giving assurances to the French Court as part of the marriage bargain
that England's anti-Catholic laws would not be enforced. Witty, gay, in love
with masques and dances—she herself would take the stage at court and
defend women performing on London's public stage—yet at the same time
devout in her religion, Queen Henrietta Maria tinged Charles's court with
both Catholicism and frivolity.

Far from healing the division between Court and Country, therefore, war
and a new monarch exacerbated division. The confrontation regularly peaked
in Parliament. In 1625, Parliament cut Charles's revenues, and rather than

vote him the traditional customs duties for life voted but a one year grant. Charles ignored the vote, claimed customs as his by right, and went on collecting the duties. The Parliament of 1626 voted no additional funds to the king but attempted to impeach Buckingham, only to be dissolved for its pains. "I would not have the House [of Commons] to question my servants, much less one that is so near me," Charles told the members. They wanted the war, he reminded them; wars required money.

> Now that you have all things according to your wishes and that I am so
> far engaged that you think there is no retreat, now you begin to set the
> dice and make your own game. But I pray you be not deceived. It is not
> a parliamentary way, nor is it a way to deal with a King. [14]

With Parliament gone he ordered that his subjects individually "lend" him the money they would have paid if the Parliament had voted funds, demanded that coastal towns provide ships for the navy at their own charge, and that the counties provide free billeting for troops being raised for another expedition. Outright resistance to these exactions, particularly to what is referred to as the "Forced Loan," was rife; men refused to pay and, in some cases were imprisoned for their refusal. An angry House of Commons in 1628 voted a surfeit of money, then bottled its bills in committee until Charles agreed to accept a "Petition of Right" declaring arbitrary taxation, arbitrary imprisonment, the billeting of soldiers in private homes, and the use of martial law to be contrary to the laws and traditions of England. But the king had the last word when, in adjourning the session, he told the members that, as he read the petition, it in no way entrenched upon his prerogatives, in the exercise of which he owed accounting "to none but to God alone."[15]

Winthrop's Place in the Conflict

What of Winthrop during these years? Few of his letters and papers remain, and these few largely deal with family matters and his legal affairs. There are hints, however.

In January of 1626 he was clearly unruffled by Charles's Catholic marriage, optimistically reporting "muche speeche of the Kinges purpose to bring the Queene to our [Protestant] church" and that "there is order given to the Bishops to proceed against the papistes by ecclesiasticall censures."[16] At the same time he was involved on the fringe of Country politics, being active to secure a seat in the forthcoming Parliament for Sir Robert Naunton, whom he described as "sounde for Religion, firme to the Common Wealth . . . and the meetest man to further the affaires of our Countrye"— "especially for our Clothiers" (Document 5-b).[17] (While the hard times of the 1620s had considerably improved in the countryside, the clothmakers of the East Anglian counties, including Suffolk, were still depressed.) But Winthrop was behind times in this nomination. Sir Robert Crane, to whom Winthrop wrote on the matter, curtly rejected the thought on behalf of the Country leaders of Bury St. Edmunds. Naunton was a former privy councillor and protege of Buckingham's; currently he was master of the King's Court of

Wards and Liveries. The leaders, Sir Robert wrote, "aleged that he was tyed in so partickiuler an obligation to his magesty as if ther was ocasion to speke for the Cuntry he wold be silent." "In Generall," he added, the leaders "wolde give no voise to anye Cortier espetialy at this time of all others."[18]

Had Winthrop misread the times? Or did his support for Naunton stem from his own desire for a profitable place in London to supplement his influence and the income of his land and law work? In any event, he seems to have been watching for just such a place in Naunton's own court. The next year (in January 1627) one of the three attornies appointed by the master to practice in the Court of Wards died suddenly. Winthrop was in Groton, but John Jr., from London, hastily conveyed the news and the advice of Emmanuel Downing, one of the surviving attornies and the husband of John's favorite sister, Lucy. "Come up with all speed you can to London," the son wrote; Naunton was out of town for the moment, and inclined to give (or more probably sell) the office to Winthrop. But he was afraid that the king or Buckingham might usurp the patronage by commanding him, before he awarded the office, to give it to another. To avoid this, Winthrop should be on hand so that he might ride out to meet the master as he returned, thus forestalling any action by king or king's favorite (Document 5-c).[19] It was, in effect, a race for office in the best Stuart tradition, one which Winthrop won.

If Winthrop was playing the game, however, the game, the times themselves, and his own very personal situation continually vexed and troubled him. His comments in letters home to Groton about specific events seem curt and laconic—"2 or 3 Londoners committed, about the Loane"[20] —but the laconic tone masked a rising dismay. Indeed, he seems to have been at least on the fringe, perhaps in the thick, of the resistance to the Forced Loan, for in December 1626, from Groton, he wrote to John Junior in London instructing him to visit the imprisoned Parliamentarian Sir Francis Barrington "and acquaint him how thinges have gone in our countye." But, he added, Junior "must doe it in private." "The good Lord blesse you . . . and guide us all wisely and faithfully in the middest of the dangers and discouragementes of these declininge tymes."[21] Friends and relatives, writing to Winthrop, were more direct. Thus in March 1627 his sister, Lucy Downing, wrote from London of "no newes but very tart: and hard standinge to knowe the liberties of our persons and goodes yet wee are verie wise an curragious."[22]

One event directly troubled Winthrop, for it touched his family. Young John himself joined one of Buckingham's overseas expeditions and the father feared for both the son's godliness in such company and his safety: be not "infected by the evill conversation of any that you may be forced to converse with. . . . be not rash upon ostentation of valor." When word of the inevitable disaster seeped back to England, John surely shared Margaret's feelings: the news of the Duke's "bad sucsese . . . put us in great feare. . . . the Lord fit and prepare us for what sover it shall please him to send to us."[23] (Young John ultimately returned safe and unharmed.) All the while, the very life he was living seemed to pall.

Four times a year Winthrop's duties at the Court of Wards called him from Groton to the city; so too did the sporadic meetings of Parliament, for he seems to have been a regular attendant at its committees. Drafts of acts "for the preventing of Drunkenness and the great wast of Graine within this Kingdome" and "to settle a Course in the Assessinge and Levienge of Common Charges in Townes and parishes" are extant among his papers.[24] True, he seems to have kept himself apart from the tumult of the city itself. He lived quietly at the home of a relative, usually that of brother-in-law Thomas Fones "att the signe of the three fawnes in the Ould Baylye"; his social contacts seem to have been limited to family, friends up from Suffolk, and acquaintances made in the law courts. Yet he disliked the city, the travel to and from Groton, and, although the profits of his attorneyship were good—"successe beyonde our expectation," he told Margaret shortly after winning the position[25]—the expense of maintaining the family in Groton and himself in London was great. In February 1628 he was contemplating either leaving his office or relocating in or near the city. He vacillated, then hesitantly decided for the latter. He must, Winthrop wrote young John (now back from the wars and in London), "take order about my removall, which I am now (in a manner) resolved off, if God shall dispose for us accordingly: for my charge heere grows verye heavye, and I am wearye of these journies to and fro, so as I will either remove or put off my office." Young John was to "enquire about for a house at tower-hill or some suche open place, or if I cant be provided so neere, I will make a tryall of [suburban] Isleworth: I would be neere churche and some good schoole" (Document 5-e).[26] He vacillated still more and within a few weeks sent Junior looking for a chamber for himself alone. But the matter was still at issue. In June of 1628 Margaret herself pressed for a house in the city. Isleworth was all right in some respects—"in regard of the good Minister an[d] good people and teachinge for our children"—but it would mean that John would likely travel to and from home by Thames River "which I know not it may be dangerous for you in the winter time the wether beinge colde and the waters perilous." "I did confir with my mother about it," Margaret added, "and she thinkes you had better take a house in the city, and so come home to your o[w]ne table and familye and I am of the same minde."[27] Still John vacillated. And in a very real way this outer vacillation seems reflective of an inward vacillation imposed on John by his Country attitudes and that Puritan conscience so long ago awakened by Culverwell and nurtured over the years by other preachers, by reading, and by introspection—a conscience we cannot forget when we consider such a man as Winthrop. He was ambitious, and ambition linked him to his attorneyship, to London, and to worldly affairs; yet he was repelled by the sinfulness of his ambition, by the city, by the world itself, and thought of Groton as the antithesis of the world.

Notes

1. Stone, *The Causes of the English Revolution: 1529-1642* (London: Routledge and Kegan Paul, 1972); Part III, idem, *The Crisis of the Aristocracy, 1558-1641*

(Oxford: Clarendon Press, 1965). See also Perez Zagorin, *The Court and the Country: The Beginning of the English Revolution* (London: Routledge and Kegan Paul, 1968).

2. Sir Anthony Denton (*ca.* 1601) and E. Waterhouse (1665) quoted in Stone, *Crisis of the Aristocracy,* pp. 387-88.

3. In *Causes of the English Revolution,* p. 105.

4. Letter of January 29, 1621/22, Mass. Hist. Soc., *Winthrop Papers,* vol. I, p. 268.

5. Quoted in Bridenbaugh, *Vexed and Troubled Englishmen,* p. 381.

6. Sir Edward Conway quoted in Finberg, ed., *Agrarian History of England and Wales,* vol. IV, p. 632.

7. Letter of December 19, 1623, Mass. Hist. Soc., *Winthrop Papers,* vol. I, p. 293.

8. Winthrop to John Winthrop, Jr., March 7, 1623/24, ibid., p. 311.

9. Ibid., pp. 295-310 prints the "Grevances." [*See Part 2, Document 4.*]

10. Crane to Winthrop, December 15, 1623, ibid., pp. 292-93.

11. See Conrad Russell, *The Crisis of Parliaments: English History, 1509-1660* (London and New York: Oxford University Press, 1971), pp. 298-99.

12. Peter Wentworth (1626) quoted in Roger Lockyer, *Tudor and Stuart Britain, 1471-1714* (New York: St. Martin's Press, 1964), p. 247.

13. Sir John Eliot, quoted in ibid., p. 248.

14. Quoted in ibid., p. 247.

15. "Proceedings on the Petition of Right (1628)," Carl Stephenson and Frederick George Marcham, eds., *Sources of English Constitutional History* (New York: Harper and Brothers, 1937), p. 453.

16. Winthrop to Margaret Winthrop, January 14, 1625/26, Mass. Hist. Soc., *Winthrop Papers,* vol. I, p. 325.

17. Ibid. See also Winthrop to Sir Robert Crane, January 14, 1625/26, ibid., pp. 324-35. [*For the latter see Part 2, Document 5-b.*] In Winthrop's terminology, "Country" and "County" were synonymous.

18. Letter of January 18, 1625/26, ibid., p. 326.

19. Letter of January 15, 1626/27, ibid., p. 340. [*See Part 2, Document 5-c.*]

20. Winthrop to Margaret Winthrop, June 15, 1627, ibid., p. 356.

21. Letter of December 18, 1626, ibid., p. 337.

22. Ibid., p. 381.

23. Winthrop to John Winthrop, Jr., June 6, 1627; Margaret Winthrop to Winthrop, n.d. but *ca.* October 1627, both in ibid., pp. 352-53, 365.

24. Ibid., pp. 373-74, 418-19.

25. Letter of *ca.* April 1627, ibid., p. 345.

26. Letter of February 25, 1627/28, ibid., p. 379. [*See Part 2, Document 5-e.*]

27. Letter to Winthrop, *ca.* June 17, 1628, ibid., pp. 400-401.

4

Calamities

To move or not move? To put off his office and remain at Groton, thus accepting financial loss and taking himself away from the center of great events, or to retain his office and remove to London, thus accepting the city and worldly ambition? It was with such a vexation—mundane yet at the same time intensely personal—that Winthrop began the year of decision: 1629.

For a Puritan—indeed, for any good Country man—the year began portentiously. The rebuff to English expeditions abroad seemed but a symptom of a general crumbling of French and German Protestantism before Catholic arms. The besieged Protestants of La Rochelle, for example, had been forced to surrender in October 1628. (The expedition in which John Junior had sailed had been meant to relieve the town's defenders, while in February 1628 Margaret had prayed that "the lord helpe them and fite for them and then none shall prevayle against them or overcome them" (Document 5-d).[1] In March 1629, the Catholic Church in Germany was restored to almost all the lands it had lost at the Reformation. In May, Denmark was forced to withdraw its support from German Protestantism.

At home, meanwhile, Charles very obviously was considering the hard-won Petition of Right little more than a scrap of paper. The customs duties were again a major problem. No Parliament since that of 1625 had voted them but the king's collectors were still attempting their collection, seizing the goods of merchants, even imprisoning recalcitrants who refused to pay. And a long-simmering controversy within the church was heating to the boiling point.

The Rise of Arminianism

The dominant mode within England's church (with Puritanism simply an exaggerated form) was generally Protestant and specifically Calvinistic. The accepted credal basis was the absolute omnipotence of God. He, by His own free will and according to His own plan, without reference to man's desires, entreaties, or actions—good or bad—saved and damned. The teaching of the church—in theory, hence regardless of whether a particular minister taught well (as the Puritan preachers described their own teaching), badly, or not at all (as the Puritan generally described the non-Puritan)—stressed the inward mystery of each individual coming to an awareness of this omnipotent God. For a long time, however, a minority among churchmen had been tending to temper this cold, hard, Calvinistic stance. They argued that while God freely offered a way to salvation, man at least had freedom to accept or reject that way. And they worked to accentuate the rich mystery and ritual of church service—the priesthood, communion, the mass—as helpful to men in coming to a decision for God. In the parlance of the time this minority position was

"Arminianism," and in the 1620s "Arminians" had come to exert more and more influence on the Court and through the Court upon the Church as a whole. Buckingham gave sporadic support to the Arminians; Charles, as king, more steadfast support. Leading Arminians (in particular William Laud) were preferred in church office. Arminian doctrine was forwarded in the universities and the old, Calvinistic doctrines prohibited as "controversial." In essence, a rising Arminianism was beginning to impose a new orthodoxy on England's church, leading one old bishop (who had conveyed England's condemnation of formal Dutch Arminianism to an international synod in 1618) to wonder bemusedly in the 1620s "why men should be restrained from teaching that doctrine hereafter, which hitherto has been generally and publicly maintained."[2]

The effect of all this was twofold. First, Arminianism in its English context was a counterreformation, a turning of England's church back toward (but not to) Catholicism. Indeed, Richard Montague, a leading Arminian elevated to a bishopric by Charles, professed in one book to reduce the points of difference between the Church of England and the Church of Rome from forty-seven to eight. To the Puritan, even simply to the staunchly Protestant Country man, this Anglo-Catholic turn was anathema. Catholicism was the great enemy to be fought abroad in Germany, Spain, France; here was a homegrown variety, taking England from within. To whatever degree Arminianism captured the Court (and by 1629 it was to a considerable degree) the split between Court and Country was so much the greater.

Second, Puritanism, being the exaggerated form of the old orthodoxy, was axiomatically the principal opponent of a rising Arminian orthodoxy. Laud, for example, as early as 1625, submitted to Buckingham a list of clergymen marked "P" and "O" (Puritan and Orthodox) as a basis for preferment in the church; subsequently a campaign to suppress the Puritan preachers rose in direct relationship to the rising power of the Arminians. Moreover, as rising Arminianism cut down the difference between orthodox England and Catholicism on the one side, it steadily increased the area of thought which Arminianism ascribed as unorthodox, ergo "Puritan" (for such was the dichotomy of labels) on the other. So rapid was the shift that a man could consider himself orthodox and proper one year and find himself considered unorthodox and Puritan the next. The Arminian, in essence, was in the position of fighting a Puritan enemy and, by definition, constantly enlarging the number of his enemies.

For the moment, however, the most immediate effect was the first—the aggravation of the Country-Court split. By the Parliamentary session of March 1629 most Country leaders were fully aroused to the danger to traditional Protestantism posed by the Arminians. A subcommittee of the House of Commons condemned Arminianism as contrary to the faith of the Church of England and all reformed, Protestant churches. At the same time, some of the leaders in the session were joining old issues to the new: if the king refused to be bound by the Petition of Right, if he persisted in illegal exactions, it was for a purpose; and if he persisted in forwarding what to the Country was the

Catholicism of the Arminians, his purpose—a return to Catholicism—seemed clear enough. Charles soon had enough of this sort of reasoning and resolved to adjourn the session. But some—the most forward—of the Country leaders would have their say. In a tumultous, unprecedented scene the king's command to adjourn was refused by the House of Commons. The doors to its meeting hall were locked and barred against the entry of the king's messenger and his knocks were ignored. The Speaker of the House was held forcibly in his chair as a symbol that the House was still in session. Tearfully the Speaker expostulated. He was but a servant of the king, and the king commanded him to rise. No! He was a servant of the House, the leaders answered, and he would "sit as long as the House pleases." In short order three resolutions were read condemning as "a capital enemy to this kingdom and commwealth" and "a betraier of the liberties of England, and an enemy of the same" anyone advising the king to collect customs duties not granted by Parliament, anyone paying such duties, and anyone seeking to "bring in innovation of religion, or by favour or countenance seek to extent or introduce popery or Arminianism, or other opinion disagreeing from the true and orthodox church."[3] Only following the acclamation of the resolutions was the Speaker released and the House adjourned. In the days following, the riotous leaders were arrested and imprisoned in the Tower of London. The king resolved to rule without Parliament—he would not summon it again for eleven years. And among Country men, confidence in the king all but disappeared.

Winthrop was not in London for this tumultous session. He had been plagued by a long, severe illness during the Hilary term of the Court of Wards (January 23 to February 12) and had gone home to Groton to recoup immediately the court recessed. But his brother-in-law Downing sent him the news posthaste, including a full description of the scene in the House and of the rumors whipping about London's streets: the arrested members "close prisoners"; "2 barges attending at Whytehall to carry some noblemen to the tower;" the Customs House doors "shutt up for that the officers dare not sett to demaund Custome;" "the Customers of Lynn . . . beaten out of the Customhowse" by a mob (Document 5-g).[4] Winthrop's immediate reaction is lost to us, but it could only have been shock, dismay, a sense of calamity.

Personal Calamity

The calamitous events in the state at large, however, were for Winthrop merely counterpoint on a higher level to calamity on a personal, family level. For his sons were failing! The quiet Country progression from father to son which Winthrop had himself experienced was not being repeated, a fact repeatedly thrust upon Winthrop during the winter and spring of 1629.

As 1629 began Winthrop could expect three of his eight children to be well on their way to taking their places in the adult world: John Junior, Henry, and Forth. But John Junior, despite his father's injunction not to return to England without "a hood at your backe," had indeed come home from Ireland and Trinity College sans degree. He had tried the law, and quickly tired of it. His soldiering at La Rochelle had been but a symptom of wanderlust. And almost as soon as he was back from the wars (November 1627) he was contemplating traveling abroad (March 1628). By mid-1628 he was in Leghorn, Italy, on an extended tour of the Mediterranean. The father who ached to hear of "any good Course for the imployment of your life and talentes"[5] knew, in early 1629, only that his eldest son was somewhere in the Levant. Junior's wanderlust, moreover, was infecting Forth. Having completed his baccalaureate at Emmanuel College, Cambridge, Forth was expected by his father to continue his studies and enter the church as a minister, fulfilling the thwarted ambition of the father. And for a while Forth agreed. But there is more than a tinge of envy in a letter to his brother, written in Latin as the latter set out on his Mediterranean journey. "We have derived different habits, and pursue a different kind of life," Forth wrote. I cling to Cambridge, "to her hallowed halls and chapels, to her sacred precepts of the Muses, and to her illustrious fountains of learning." You labor "with the desire of seeing unknown lands, and of beholding strange customs." When "I enter on a longer journey than you have undertaken, it is only among my books. . . . Here I am fixed, and such is the fortune of my life." He was not as fixed as he imagined, however. Some time in the spring of 1629 he left Cambridge for Groton, and there he tarried while Winthrop wondered what his son was about.[6] By June, Forth's Cambridge tutor was complaining that his long absence "doth him much hurte, both in his learninge and manners," leading John to complain to Margaret: "I praye thee speake with him, and doe as may be fittest, for if he intendes not the ministerye, I have no greate minde to send him any more; if he doth, let him goe as soone as he can."[7]

Above all, Winthrop's second son, Henry, was failing. At eighteen (December 1626) he had sailed for the West Indies and the Island of Barbados to make his fortune as a tobacco planter. But it was soon obvious that the venture was disastrous. Henry's ambition was large; his debts (sent to Winthrop for payment) substantial; and the tobacco he dispatched back almost worthless—"verye ill conditioned, fowle, full of stalkes and evill coloured," wrote Winthrop. In January 1629, while Winthrop was fretful about his own long illness and about the prospects for his younger children should he die, he received a request from Henry for still more assistance. "I doe wonder upon what grounde you should be ledd into so gross an error," he responded angrily, "as to thinke, that I could provide 10: such men [servants] as you write for and disburse a matter of 200 *li* (when I owe more allreadye, then I am able to paye, without sale of my land) and to doe this at some 2: or 3: monthes warninge. . . . I have many other children that are unprovided, and I see my life is uncertain. I marvaile at your great undertakeinges, havinge no meanes. . . . this hathe been allwayes the fruit of your vaine, overreachinge minde, which wilbe your overthrowe, if you attaine not more discreation and moderation" (Document 5-f).[8]

Henry never received this letter. As it was being written he was already on his way back to England and sometime that spring he appeared in London. To save him "from much expence and rioutous company," Uncle Thomas

Fones took him in. But the "rioutous company" came along with him. Fones complained to Winthrop that "yf he were within my howse [it] was like an Inne." Among the company was even "a papist," although Uncle Thomas gave him short shrift once he learned of visits to a priest in nearby Newgate. And how had Henry repaid his uncle for all this kindness and endurance? He "hath wooed and wonne my daughter Besse for a wyfe and they both pretend to have proceeded so far that there is no recallying of yt." To Fones a marriage was clearly unsuitable. "I will not multiply argumentes agaynst my Nephew being your sonne," he wrote Winthrop; "but his hart I see is much to bigg for his estates." (In other words, Henry could not afford to marry.) Fones's protests to Henry, however, were met by "braving opposition" of a sort he would not take if he himself were not deathly ill and the boy was not Winthrop's son.

> I cannot write yow the many trobles of my mind . . . for my Nephew sayes playnly yf he cannot have my good will to have my daughter he will have her without: and though I have entreated him to forbeare my howse a while he will not but comes and stayes at unfitting howres. . . . I am weak and cannot I see now be master in myne owne howse. . . . I long to heare from yow for I doubt [not] he will draw hir forth of mine owne howse and soddaynly marry hir without any Scruples (Document 5-h).[9]

Winthrop hurried to London in response to Fones's plea, but by then there was little to be done. The incident was too much for Fones—he died April 15, shortly after writing Winthrop. Ten days later Henry and Elizabeth were married and packed off to Groton, Winthrop warning Margaret to keep Henry home "as much as thou canst," particularly from the taverns and inns of the larger towns about Groton. "Be not dismayed at the crosses thou meetest with in familye affaires," he added, reflecting his own dismay; "flye to him, who will take up thy burden for thee, goe thou on cheerfully in obedience to his holy will."[10]

In Winthrop's mind, calamity for the Protestant cause abroad, calamity in Parliament, and calamity in his own family could only merge and reinforce each other. The family, he would write at another time and in another context, was a little commonwealth, and a commonwealth a greater family; quiet deference and attention to responsibility should mark both.[11] But the irresoluteness of Junior and Forth and the dissoluteness of Henry seemed to put in question his own performance of fatherly responsibility. And where was deference within the family when Henry put up "braving opposition" to Uncle Thomas and deprived him of the mastery of his own house? In the larger family (the commonwealth of England) the king was clearly failing his responsibility as father within the kingdom, but when the king's children turned against his authority—as the Commons did on the tumultous last day of Parliament—the children were equally failing in their proper deference. And God, as the father of all those gathered in the Protestant churches of Europe, was obviously turning his back on his children, surrendering them to Satan and Catholicism. This last could only be deserved punishment meted out on children, for at least in this one case the father (God) could do no wrong. What then, Winthrop could ask himself, of his own faults? his children's? the king's? the Parliamentarians'? Indeed, what of the myriad of England's social faults—those that he had cited in the despondent days of 1622 when he took part in writing the "Grevances Groaning for Reformation," the consciousness of which seemed to have rushed back on him now? What of the sinful ways of the Court, so anathema to a good Country man yet so infectious—Henry's invasion of the Fones's home and seduction of the daughter of the house could not but remind Winthrop of Court behavior! What of the sinful turn of England's leaders toward Arminianism and Catholicism? Their rejection of the Godly preachers? Was not all of this deserving of God's punishment, of God's "Scquorge and Judgment" upon his English children, his *favorite* children. Two weeks after Henry's marriage to Elizabeth Fones, four weeks after the closing of Parliament, all of Winthrop's fear and frustration—and a glimmer of hope—poured out in a letter to Margaret. "The Lorde hath admonished, threatened, corrected, and astonished us, yet we growe worse and worse," he wrote; having smitten the Protestant churches of the continent for their sins—letting them fall to Catholic arms—God must surely turn on a sinful England. Yet must His fury be borne by all in the kingdon? Perhaps not. "If the Lord seeth it wilbe good for us, he will provide a shelter and a hidinge place for us and ours" (Document 5-i).[12]

"A hidinge place." What was on Winthrop's mind as he wrote the phrase? Probably Winthrop himself did not have a firm idea at this point in time (May 15). Certainly he seems immediately to have resolved the vexing question with which he began the year—retain his office and remove to the city, or put off his office and his ambitions. Now there was no more talk of moving to London. Indeed, he seems immediately involved in negotiations to rid himself of his attorneyship in the Court of Wards—in this day of patronage, quitting was a delicate procedure. On June 5, to Margaret, he wrote that he thought his office was gone "so as I shall not wronge thee so much with my absence as I have done." On June 19 he wrote that his only news was that "my Office is gone, and my chamber [in London], and I shalbe a saver in them both: so as I hope, we shall now enjoye each other againe as we desire."[13] But if his office—and with it the city—was gone, was it in his mind to retreat to the Country and Groton? That was the alternative of 1628, and his assurances to Margaret that he would be with her more often than before implies that it was the alternative of 1629. Perhaps, however, he had it in mind to retreat even farther.

Notes

1. Margaret Winthrop to Winthrop, *ca.* February 4, 1627/28, Mass. Hist. Soc., *Winthrop Papers*, vol. II, p. 59. [*See Part 2, Document 5-d*]

2. John Davenant, Bishop of Salisbury, quoted in Russell, *Crisis of Parliaments*, p. 214.

3. Ibid., p. 309; "Resolutions of the Commons (1629)," Stephenson and Marcham, eds., *Sources*, pp. 454-55.

4. Letter of March 6, 1628/29, Mass. Hist. Soc., *Winthrop Papers*, vol. II, pp. 74-75. [*See Part 2, Document 5-g*]

5. Winthrop to John Winthrop, Jr., February 22, 1624/25, ibid., vol. I, p. 318.

6. Ibid., pp. 393-94.

7. Winthrop to Margaret Winthrop, June 5, 1629, ibid., vol. II. p. 94.

8. Winthrop to Henry Winthrop, January 30, 1629, ibid., pp. 67-68. [*See Part 2, Document 5-f.*]

9. Thomas Fones to Winthrop, April 2, 1629, ibid., pp. 78-79. [*See Part 2, Document 5-h.*]

10. Letter of April 28, 1629, ibid., p. 84.

11. In a declaration to the Massachusetts Bay General Court in 1637, ibid., vol. III, pp. 422 *ff.*

12. Letter of May 15, 1629, ibid., p. 91. [*See Part 2, Document 5-i*]

13. Ibid., pp. 94, 99-100.

5

Places to Hide

Clearly Winthrop, by the late spring of 1629, was discontented, alienated, in England. He had begun the year already poised between the city and Country Groton; events during the early months of the year—abroad, in Parliament, within his family—together with his conviction that the calamities presaged God's "Scquorge and Judgment," could only exaggerate his desire to retreat. He was, in a word, *vulnerable*—vulnerable specifically to the question "shall I leave England?" *if* indeed that question were either put to him or had occurred to him of itself. Yet vulnerability alone is not enough to explain Winthrop's decision to leave England, let alone his decision for America. If he had no knowledge of alternatives to his English condition, if he could not conceive of any other retreat than Groton, the question "shall I leave?" would not have occurred to him, nor made much sense if put to him. It is to Groton that he would have withdrawn and in all likelihood he would have been lost to history. Our question follows from these considerations: of what hiding places, other than Groton, might Winthrop have knowledge in this spring of 1629.

We can certainly presume a broad general knowledge of the world on the part of Winthrop, for his maturing years had coincided with a spectacular growth of geographic knowledge among educated Englishmen, a steady widening of England's overseas commerce, and the first settlement of Englishmen in America. The year after his birth the first edition of Richard Hakluyt's *Principall Navigations, Voiages and Discoveries of the English Nation* was published, one of the most important of all English books for its effect in expanding geographical horizons. Here were accounts and descriptions of the Russian plains, Africa, the commerce of the Near and Far East, the discoveries in the Americas. When Winthrop was three years old the first Englishmen were trading in India; he was twelve when the greatest of England's overseas commercial companies—the East India Company—was chartered. When he was nineteen, married, and a father, Englishmen first settled on the banks of the James River in Virginia. The London in which he spent so much time in the 1620s was principally a seaport. Warehouses crowded its streets and alleys, merchants its walkways, and ships from Antwerp and Amsterdam, Hamburg and Archangel, Constantinople and Bengal—indeed, from all about the world—crowded the anchorage and docks of Thames River. And the crowded Thames led to lands his sons had already seen (or were seeing in 1629): Junior to Ireland, La Rochelle, and now to the Mediterranean; Henry to the Caribbean. By their own travels the sons widened still further the geographic knowledge of the father.

Most of this world beyond England Winthrop undoubtedly knew only in terms of strange lands where Englishmen carried goods to be bought and sold—extensions of the city, so to speak, not places in which to hide. We can, however, presume Winthrop knew specifically of the Netherlands as a place of refuge for some of the Puritan preachers. William Ames, one of the most prominent of the preachers, had spent a part of his boyhood in the village of Boxford a mile from Groton; as a minister he had occasionally preached in Boxford before being silenced by the bishops and (in 1610) leaving for Holland. Winthrop's father recorded hearing Ames preach in 1607; John undoubtedly heard him as well and knew of his place of exile. Perhaps, too, Winthrop knew of the independent congregations Englishmen had established in the Netherlands—radical religionists who had chosen to break completely from the English church and pursue their own course. Was a hiding place to be found in the Netherlands? Probably not. Winthrop was not truly radical in religious matters. He could not conceive of leaving the English church but felt only that the church hierarchy, in its trend toward Arminianism, was leaving him. Moreover, the Dutch were at war with Spain. To move in their direction would be to move toward God's maelstrom, not away. In the Netherlands, moreover, was to be found an overtaxed economy and a settled culture. Could an English family maintain its English traditions there? The Pilgrims of Plymouth, who had in part sojourned in Leyden, thought not, Nathaniel Morton giving as one of their reasons for departing for America in 1620 the fear "that their Posterity would in few generations become *Dutch*, and so lose their interest in the *English* Nation."[1]

We know, too, that Winthrop had direct knowledge of English settlements in Ireland. His Uncle John had gone there shortly after Winthrop's birth; Londoners sponsored systematic settlement in Ulster from 1611 on; Winthrop's brother-in-law Emmanuel Downing owned land in Ireland (the link which led John Junior to attend Trinity College, Dublin rather than Cambridge); and in the pessimistic days of 1622 and 1623, in a letter to Junior, Winthrop had remarked that he often wished "God would open a waye to settle me in Ireland, if it might be for his glorye."[2] Ireland might well have been a conjectured hiding place in 1629.

Finally, we can presume that by 1629 Winthrop had knowledge of America. England's first entry into Virginia in 1607 had been followed by years of straggling, erratic development there and (after 1612) on Bermuda. But in the 1620s the effort began to bloom. A broad campaign undertaken on behalf of Virginia resulted in the dispatch of some three thousand new settlers between 1619 and 1622. The Caribbean was entered as Englishmen settled on St. Christopher's in the Leeward Islands (1624) and on Barbados (1627). In 1620 the Leyden Pilgrims, sailing for Virginia, made land by accident at Cape Cod and settled at Plymouth in New England. The private Council for New England began sponsoring settlements in 1622 along what would become the Maine and New Hampshire coast. In 1624, led by their Puritan preacher, John White, a group of Dorchester merchants sponsored a fishing station on Cape Ann to the north of what is now Boston. The Cape

Ann settlement languished and in 1626 the Dorchester sponsors disbanded. But preacher White persevered, seeking support among Puritan laymen elsewhere in England. In 1628 the "New England Company for a Plantation in Massachusetts Bay" was organized, its membership consisting of some of the old Dorchester investors, a few country gentlemen, and (for the most part) London merchants and lawyers—all with a definite Puritan cast. The same year an expedition under John Endecott reinforced and reinvigorated the settlement in New England, now named Salem. The following year the undertakers reorganized and obtained a royal charter as "the Governor and Company of Massachusetts Bay in New England."[3]

Early Visions of America

Winthrop's personal involvement in any of these ventures prior to 1629 was only indirect and largely through his sons. We have already noted Henry's sojourn in the Caribbean. The ill success of Henry's tobacco venture, however, would hardly incline Winthrop to envision a hiding place in either Virginia or the Caribbean. More important was the gathering together in the New England Company of so many Puritan laymen, some of them among Winthrop's circle of London friends and acquaintances, which brought the New England efforts very close to him. There was talk of the company and of the Endecott voyage in the Fones and Downing households, particularly the latter, for Downing had a vague relationship to the company, perhaps even as an investor. The talk seems to have caught the imagination of footloose Junior in the early months of 1628. His notion that he might join the expedition, dutifully passed on to Winthrop, undoubtedly informed the father of New England but hardly enthused him: "I know not wheare you should goe with such religious company and under such hope of blessinge, onely I am loth you should thinke of settlinge there. . . . Be advised by your uncle [Downing] and other your worthy freindes who are experienced in these affaires."[4] (In the end, of course, Junior went off to the Mediterranean instead.) But as thoughts of New England continued to circulate in his family and among his friends, an inchoate image formed in Winthrop's mind.

Obviously we cannot enter into Winthrop's mind to see this image for ourselves; neither can we overhear the stray conversations of 350 years ago which might have formed it, nor do we know for certain what he read about New England. But the shadow of that image can perhaps be discerned in the pamphlets and broadsides which circulated in the 1620s in support of American plantations in general and New England settlement in particular. In 1622, for example, there appeared from the printers *A Relation or Journall of the . . . English Plantation Setled at Plimoth in New England*, to which was appended a letter from the Pilgrim deacon Robert Cushman on "the Lawfulness of Removing out of England into the Parts of America." Richard Eburne's *A Plaine Path-way to Plantations* appeared in 1624, together with Edward Winslow's *Good Newes from New-England*, reporting on Plymouth, and John Smith's *Generall Historie of Virginia, New-England, and the*

Summer Isles [Bermuda]—the last appearing in six editions prior to 1629. John Bellamy's *An Historical Discoverie and Relation of the British Plantations in New England* was published in 1627. In 1628 Christopher Levett's *A Voyage into New England* described the northern coast.

The thrust of all these pamphlets was much the same, for in the 1620s an earlier image of America as a lush, languid, easy land—a sixteenth-century image owing more to Spanish accounts of the Caribbean and South America than to English activities along the North American coast—was being overlaid by the image of a land offering ready reward to those who worked. "I will not do . . . as some have done, to my knowledge speake more than is true," Levett wrote; "I will not tell you that you may smell the corne-fields before you see the Land; neither must men think that corne doth grow naturally (or on trees), nor will the Deare come when they are called . . . nor the fish leap into a kettle." If any have such ideas, they had best stay at home. But for men of "great spirits and small meanes," to quote Smith, "who [among such] can desire more content . . . then to tread and plant that ground he hath purchased by the hazard of his life; if hee have but the taste of vertue and magnanimity, what to such a minde can bee more pleasant then planting and building a foundation for his posterity, got from the rude earth by Gods blessing and his owne industry?"[5] America's opportunity was regularly contrasted with an image of an England beset by social ills and bereft of opportunity for all but a few. Cushman's letter in the *Relation . . . of . . . Plimoth*—a letter which, on the basis of a comparison with Winthrop's later writings we can suspect he read—put the contrast succinctly. In England "each man is fain to pluck his means, as it were, out of his nieghbour's throat."

> There is such pressing and oppressing, in town and country, about farms, trades, traffic, etc.; so as a man can hardly anywhere set up a trade, but he shall pull down two of his neighbors. The towns abound with young tradesmen and the hospitals are full of the ancient. The country is replenished with new farmers; and the almhouses are filled with old labourers. Many there are who get their living with bearing burdens; but more are fain to burden the land with their whole bodies. Multitudes get their means of life by prating [trickery], and so do numbers more, by begging.

Comparison "with the easiness, plainness, and plentifulness in living" in America, the writer continued, "may quickly persuade any man to a liking of this course, and to practice a removal" (Document 6).[6]

Removal, moreover, promising benefits to the individual, was also put forth as a service to the kingdom and to God. Given a belief that England was overpopulated, the departure of some Englishmen and their prospering elsewhere could only improve the condition of the community of all Englishmen. "It be the people that makes the Land English, not the Land the People," Eburne wrote. Therefore,

> bee not too much in love with that countrie wherein you were borne, that countrie which bearing you . . . is indeed, weary of you. Shee accounts you a burthen to her, an encombrance to her. You keepe her down, you hurt her and make her poore and bare. . . . Take and reckon that for your Country where you may best live and thrive.[7]

Smith echoed the theme but shifted the emphasis from the negative (England would benefit by the departure of her excess) to the positive (England would benefit by their efforts in creating new English societies overseas): "What so truly sutes with honour and honesty, as . . . erecting Townes, peopling Countries, informing the ignorant, reforming things unjust, teaching vertue and gaine[ing] to our native mother Country a Kingdome to attend her." Bellamy went still a step further. The overseas societies could be conscious improvements on England. "For such as are truly Pious," he wrote, addressing himself directly to Puritan concerns, there is in New England "the opportunity to put in practise the workes of piety, both in building of Churches, and Raising of Colledges for the breeding of youth, or maintenance of Divines [ministers] and other learned men." All, however, made the point that the work to be done was God's work, for inasmuch as the English were (in the English mind) the favored people of God, the beneficial transplantation of the English—together with whatever the English could do to bring the "savages" of America to a knowledge of Christianity—was a service rendered to God. The work was not easy—a constant refrain! Wanting money to rent a house in England, Winslow wrote, a man might consider America; but he should remember that "as he shall have no rent to pay, so he must build his house before he have it." The argument (of hard work, even shortages) was easily turned, particularly by those with a Puritan cast of mind. The work was honest, virtuous, contributory to good character; shortages were merely the absence of debilitating luxuries. It was a positive good for men not to "take so much thought for the flesh as not to be pleased except they can pamper their bodies with variety of dainties."[8]

For Winthrop, so distraught in 1629 by his, his family's, his England's condition, the general thrust of this literature (and of the talk of New England which it both precipitated and reflected) could only ring true. Indeed, he would draw on all these ideas when he put in order—rationalized is the word we shall use—his reasons for leaving old England for new. So too with regard to specific themes. When Smith spoke directly to "you fathers that are either so foolishly fond, or so miserably covetous, or so wilfully ignorant, or so negligently carelesse" as to allow sons to grow up idly (urging them to send their sons to America), or Cushman of children who could not attain the good life of their fathers because "some circumventor or other will outstrip them, and make them sit in the dust," Winthrop perforce thought of *his* sons.[9] When Cushman cited among England's ills the plethora of "suits in law" or "the bitter contention that hath been about Religion," he was citing what to Winthrop were obvious and daily concerns.[10] When the publicists noted the hard work and scarcities of America as a character-building renunciation of ease and luxury, Winthrop could read a renunciation of worldliness and breathe a quiet "Amen." Above all, when the publicists wrote of removal as a service to England and God, Winthrop could seize upon the theme. True, he was in retreat, but his Puritan conscience (and, one suspects, his inclination toward worldly honors and preferment) required him to serve in the world and, through the world, serve God to the best of his abilities. Withdrawal to neither Groton nor Ireland had about it the aura of service which surrounded withdrawal to America. America it would be, then, the hiding place where still he could well serve God and his fellow Englishmen.

Notes

1. Nathaniel Morton, *New Englands Memoriall* (Cambridge: J. Usher, 1669), p. 3.

2. Letter of April 20, 1623, Mass. Hist. Soc., *Winthrop Papers*, vol. I, p. 281.

3. For these activities see Charles M. Andrews, *The Colonial Period of American History* (New Haven: Yale University Press, 1934-38) and John E. Pomfret, *Founding the American Colonies, 1583-1660* (New York: Harper and Row, 1970).

4. Winthrop to John Winthrop, Jr., April 7, 1628, Mass. Hist. Soc., *Winthrop Papers*, vol. I, p. 385. Some—*e.g.*, the editors of *Winthrop Papers;* William G. Robbins, "The Massachusetts Bay Company: An Analysis of Motives," *The Historian*, 52 (1968-70): 92—accept an obscure reference to an investment in a letter to Winthrop of April 1629 as evidence of Winthrop's involvement in the Massachusetts venture prior to the summer of 1629. It is slim evidence, however, and runs counter to the general ignorance implied in the passage quoted here.

5. Christopher Levett, *A Voyage into New England* (London: William Iones, 1628), p. 22; John Smith, *The Generall Historie of Virginia, New-England, and the Summer Isles* as reprinted in Edward Arber, ed., *Travels and Works of Captain John Smith* (Edinburgh: J. Grant, 1910), vol. II, p. 722.

6. *A Relation or Journall of the Beginning and Proceedings of the English Plantation Setled at Plimoth in New England* (London, 1622), reprinted in Edward Arber, ed., *The Story of the Pilgrim Fathers, 1606-1623* (Boston and New York: Houghton Mifflin, 1897), pp. 503-05. [*See Part 2, Document 6.*]

7. Richard Eburne, *A Plaine Path-way to Plantations* (London: John Marriott, 1624), p. A2.

8. Smith, *Generall Historie*, pp. 722-23; Bellamy as quoted in Bridenbaugh, *Vexed and Troubled Englishmen*, pp. 406-7; E[dward] W[inslow], *Good Newes from New-England* (London, 1624) as reprinted in Arber, ed., *Story of the Pilgrim Fathers*, p. 597; *Relation . . . of . . . Plimoth*, p. 504 [Document 6].

9. Smith, *Generall Historie*, p. 725; *Relation . . . of . . . Plimoth*, p. 505 [Document 6].

10. Ibid., pp. 502, 503.

6

Decision

Winthrop was vulnerable in the spring of 1629 to the question "shall I leave England." The question was logical, for there was a known alternative to England: New England. His vulnerability and the alternative came together and he arrived at his personal decision for America. The process was not, however, a sudden dawning. To the contrary, his activities and letters during the spring—the latter frequently cryptic, our knowledge of the former incomplete—suggest a relatively slow evolution.

Let us pick up Winthrop's trail (and the evidence) as he is in London dealing with the problems of the Fones household: Henry's affair with Elizabeth, Uncle Thomas's death. Having seen the marriage through and the newlyweds off to Groton, Winthrop himself remained in the city for the Easter term of the Court of Wards (April 22 to May 18). He put in motion the necessary steps to divest himself of his attorneyship, finally accomplishing this in mid-June. Quitting the court is most often considered in the light of Winthrop's subsequent emigration but, as we have seen, he had thought of quitting earlier in the context of a retreat to Groton. His quitting at this time, therefore, need not necessarily be associated with his New England decision.

The notion of a possible hegira of Puritan gentlemen was very much in the air, however, having taken form suddenly in the aftermath of the closing of Parliament, and ultimately reaching into the Tower of London where the imprisoned Parliamentarians heard of it. The precise origin of the notion, even whether it originated with one or spontaneously with several, is unknown. Clearly, the idea did not originate with Winthrop. Equally clearly, it seems to have been pressed most vigorously by a Lincolnshire circle of Puritan gentlemen centered on the household of the Earl of Lincoln, and particularly by Isaac Johnson, a brother-in-law of the Earl.[1] Moreover, John Humphrey, a Dorchester parishioner of minister John White, seems central in spreading the idea. Active in the New England affair from the time of its Dorchester beginning in the early 1620s, he seems to have carried knowledge of America into Lincolnshire as a close friend and soon-to-be (1630) brother-in-law of the Earl, inspiring Lincolnshire investment in the New England Company. Active in London as a member of the company and as a lawyer—indeed, he was the third of the attornies at the Court of Wards—he seems to have linked in thoughts of emigration the Lincolnshire group and some of the company's London leaders, including Sir Richard Saltonstall, master of one of the great London mercantile companies and nephew and heir of a lord mayor of the city, and attorney John White (no relation to minister White) who probably drafted the document which transformed the New England Company into the royally chartered Massachusetts Bay Company. Winthrop's own links to those talking of emigration were threefold: to Humphrey directly through the Court of Wards, of course; personally to attorney John White—Winthrop and White were appointed coguardians of Thomas Fones's children; and, through his own brother-in-law (and colleague at the court), Emmanuel Downing, to various Londoners involved in the company.

Winthrop, Downing, and attorney White at least—probably with others—clearly discussed emigration to New England during the Easter term of the court. But every indication is that it was at the time only a possibility to Winthrop and that he did not come to any conclusion. It is improbable, for example, that he would have decided to emigrate without his sons coming with him, yet on April 28 and again on May 1 he indicated to Margaret that Henry and his new wife were to return to Barbados and Henry's plantation there, while in early June he wrote that Forth was to return to Cambridge if he so desired.[2]

As the term ended and the court recessed to meet again during Trinity (June 5 to June 24), Winthrop delayed his departure from London. We do not know why. But he was briefly at Groton sometime between May 25 and the reopening of the court. During the visit home he probably discussed emigration with Margaret and at least one neighbor. For back in London he wrote cryptically to Margaret (June 5) that he was "still more confirmed in that Course which I propounded to thee"—presumably while he was in Groton—"and so are my brother and sister D[owning], the good Lo: direct and blesse us in it."[3] The "course" was emigration to America, but the implication that his mind was set is deluding. More to the point is neighbor Thomas Motte's letter *to* Winthrop of a few days later. He (Motte) was "inclinable" to emigration "though I heare of great rubbs in the way."

> I would very gladly talke with Mr. White if soe be I could by any meanes meete him at London. for I have many doubts and quaestions in the which I desier to be resolved and because he hath a great strooke in the plantation I suppose noe man so fitt to resolve me as he is; specially since he meaneth for to goe himselfe.[4]

The letter tends to indicate the direction of the suggestion to emigrate: through White to Winthrop to Motte. It also indicates that, to Winthrop, White (not he) was central to the project at the moment, that White (not he) was committed. Another letter, from Winthrop to Margaret on June 22, indicates the continued uncertainty in Winthrop's mind: although no longer associated with the Court of Wards he could not return to Groton at the moment, he wrote; Margaret "must have pacience till the ende of next weeke. . . . After that, I hope, we shall never parte so longe againe, till we parte for a better meetinge in heaven. but where we shall spende the rest of our short tyme [on earth], I knowe not."[5] As before, when the choice was Groton or the city, Winthrop was hesitant, vacillating.

The Final Commitment

While Winthrop hesitated, events moved on apace. By late June both Isaac Johnson and Attorney White seem committed to emigration (although in the end White would not go); one suspects that by late July there were others as well, among them Sir Richard Saltonstall. A serious sticking point had arisen and its resolution had at least begun. English overseas ventures—with the New England venture thus far no exception—had involved the dispatch of settlers overseas financed by investors remaining in England. The investors, in the interest of protecting their money, had almost invariably retained control over the settlers abroad. When, for example, John Endecott sailed to Salem in 1628, he went as a company-appointed governor of the overseas settlement, carried with him instructions from the company, and was required to report his and the settlers' activities to the company. Had those activities displeased the investors gathered in the company, they would have recalled him and sent another governor in his stead. For the Puritan gentlemen contemplating emigration, this structure was impossible. They were gentlemen well used to governing their own affairs and, as manor lords, justices of the peace, and parliamentary constituents (if not actual members of Parliament), governing others as well. They would not hazard themselves abroad if they were to be no more than servants of the company. It is obvious that this difficulty was carried by the gentlemen to the offices of the company, obvious too that a particular solution was contemplated, for on July 28 Mathew Craddock, the then-governor of the company, presented a proposition to its membership in a meeting at London:

> That for the advancement of the plantacion [in New England, and] the inducing & encouraging persons of worth & qualitie [to] transplant themselves and famylyes thether . . . to transferr the government of the plantacion to those that shall inhabite there, and not to continue the same in subordinacion to the Company here, as now it is.[6]

Craddock's proposition was not acted upon at the meeting, but it laid the seeds for subsequent events.

All the while, those who were committed pressured others—including Winthrop—to commit themselves. Sometime prior to July 8 Isaac Johnson came down from Lincolnshire to London. We know he was in contact with Downing, presumably also with Winthrop; certainly, either directly or through Downing, Johnson sought to obtain Winthrop's agreement to emigration. Downing and Winthrop apparently agreed to ride to Lincolnshire for a further conference sometime in the near future, for on his return home Johnson wrote to press for a specific date, conveying his "entreatyes" to "send mee word when it will bee and where." In the same letter Johnson noted the recent commencement at Cambridge University and the gathering there of a host of Puritan preachers to hear Minister White's "call" for support for the New England project. "It had beene an excellent Tyme for mr. Winthrope to have been" there, he added.[7] Winthrop and Downing finally left for Tattershall in late July. We know because on the road, somewhere near Ely, Winthrop's horse fell in a bog and threw him, a fact he dutifully noted in his "Experiencia" under date of July 28—the very day of Craddock's proposal in London. But Winthrop rode northward to be convinced to join the emigration, not as part of an already committed group. Behind in London his sister Lucy Downing—writing on August 8 to John Junior, then in the Netherlands on his way home—knew of no decision on

Winthrop's part when she passed along news of the family. Forth had decided to go to New England rather than return to the University, she reported. But Henry was still to return to Barbados. As for Winthrop, Lucy could only write that he was in Lincolnshire and that he "earnestlie desiers to see you."[8]

What was said at Tattershall? What arguments were used? Again, we do not know for sure. But to judge from Winthrop's later writings, the Tattershall group argued the righteousness of the venture in the same terms as had the publicists (God and England would be served) and stressed the potential for service that would be open to Winthrop personally in New England. Whatever the nature of the conversations, they were decisive. Winthrop's decision to go was evident immediately upon his return to Groton in early August. Then he seems to have put the matter to his family. Margaret undoubtedly acquiesced readily. Even when New England was simply a possibility, she seems to have responded in Biblical terms—"Whither thou goest, I will go"—prompting Winthrop to write her at one point that it was his comfort "that thou are willinge to be my companion in what place or condition soever in weale or in woe."[9] Of his grown sons, Forth was already committed to the journey—Lucy's letter of August 8 tells us that. Henry, as was his wont, might well have argued the point and been overborne. Margaret had never liked the idea of his returning to Barbados, writing subsequently that "his stay from Barbatus . . . be good. it had bin [a] pittye he should have gon to have indangered the good of his soul, by beinge partaker of the sines of the rest of that wicked company."[10] John Junior, again in England by mid-August, learned of the decision in a letter from his father and responded from London on August 21. "I shall call that my Countrie where I may most glorifie God and enjoy the presence of my dearest freindes," he wrote. "Therefore heerin I submit my selfe to Godes wil, and yours, and with your leave doe dedicate my selfe . . . to the service of God, and the Company."[11] Five days later Winthrop and eleven other Puritan gentlemen met at Cambridge to put their signatures to a formal agreement:

> For the better encourragement of ourselves and others that shall joyne with us in this action, and to the end that every man may without scruple dispose of his estate and afayres as may best fitt his preparacion for this voyage, It is fully and faithfully agreed amongst us . . . that we will so really endevour the prosecucion of this worke, as by Gods assistaunce we will be ready in our persons, and with such of our severall familyes as are to go with us and such provisions as we are able conveniently to furnish ourselves withall, to embarke for the said plantacion [in New England] by the first of March next.[12]

Notes

1. Most historians assume that the idea originated within this Lincolnshire group.
2. Mass. Hist. Soc., *Winthrop Papers*, vol. II, pp. 84, 87, 94.
3. Ibid., p. 94.
4. Of *ca*. June 13, 1629, ibid., p. 97.
5. Ibid., p. 100.
6. Nathaniel B. Shurtleff, ed., *Records of the Governor and Company of the Massachusetts Bay in New England*, vol. I (Boston: W. White, 1853), p. 49.

7. Johnson to Downing, July 8, 1629, Mass. Hist. Soc., *Winthrop Papers,* vol. II, pp. 102-3.

8. Ibid., pp. 103, 104-5.

9. Letter of June 22, 1629, ibid., p. 100.

10. Margaret to Winthrop, October 13, 1629, ibid., p. 158.

11. Ibid., p. 151.

12. Ibid., p. 151-52.

7

Rationali-
zation

His private decision made, Winthrop became a public man. As we shall see, he soon moved into a central position within the Massachusetts Bay Company, being elected governor in October. But no sooner had he returned to Groton from Lincolnshire than he issued a call for a meeting of the gentlemen of the county to take place at Bury St. Edmunds on August 12. At the same time he set to work preparing (and distributing) his notes for the meeting, setting forth a rationalization both for the New England venture and for his own participation.[1]

In the context of the time and of Winthrop's mind, this public rationalization was necessary. On one level, of course, it was incumbent upon Winthrop, as a committed member of the emigrating group, to solicit support for the project in general and, in particular, additional gentlemen emigrants. But there was another level. Winthrop had struggled to his decision in the relative privacy of his family and a small circle of friends and acquaintances. Yet he lived in a larger society of Country gentlemen, many of them lay Puritans like himself; most, if not all, thoroughly disillusioned by events (albeit those events were underscored for Winthrop by the situation within his family). Some were retreating into antiquarianism, forgetting a displeasing present in the pleasure of "the judicious understanding . . .of elder times."[2] Others were steeling themselves with a resolution to resist what they discerned as the evils abroad, to stand for godly ways and the Country's good—a steeling which, in the 1640s, would lead to revolution, civil war, and the trial and execution of King Charles. Only a few, like Winthrop, were moved to emigration. The reaction to events, in a phrase, was not monolithic, not singular, but disparate, and Winthrop's reaction was in many ways the most drastic.[3]

Winthrop had convinced himself as to this drastic course but being a man he must, as any man, establish the rectitude of his decision in terms of his peers. And to his peers—his fellow gentlemen—the questions were axiomatic. Was the venture justified in terms of God's will—in this God-serving age, and among these God-serving men, the first and most appropriate question? Was it a service or a disservice to the community of England for gentlemen of such standing and ability as Winthrop to leave? Was it not a more godly, more proper role for men such as he to remain where God had placed them, working to reform their native country? By what right did they leave their own land and enter the land of another people (the American Indian)? What of the hazards of the journey? The hardships of a new settlement? Was the venture not more proper for the young and for the common sort than for a gentleman of age and standing?[4] As Winthrop sat down to compose his notes in preparation for the Bury meeting, he addressed himself to his peers and their questions. His intent was a logical presentation, and for this he obviously drew upon his conversations of the immediate past months—conversations in which the questions had undoubtedly been asked and privately resolved—and on the publicists whose works he had read.

Winthrop considered first the very rectitude of a New England plantation, asking in effect "why should any of us go?" then turned his attention to himself, asking "why should I go?" (Documents 7 and 8).[5]

Antichrist (the Papacy) was abroad and victorious, he wrote in answer to the first. As in his letter to Margaret of mid-May he noted that "all other [Protestant] Churches of Europe are brought to desolation"; "the like Judgment is comminge upon us"; "in all places of the worlde" the Papacy is laboring to rear up its "kingdom." In this situation "who knows, but that God hathe provided this place, to be a refuge for manye, whom he meanes to save out of the general destruction." But where his earlier letter had reflected only a fearful hope for a refuge, he must now rationalize in positive terms the building of that refuge. "It wilbe a service to the [Protestant] Churche of great Consequence" to build in New England "a bullwarke" against Catholicism. And "if suche as are knowne to be godly . . . runne the hazard" in the venture, it will be "an example of greate use," giving "more life to the Faithe of Godes people" everywhere. He added, too, the secular argument of the pamphleteers. England was overpopulated. The "lande growes wearye of her Inhabitantes, so as man which is the most pretious of all Creatures, is heere more vile and base, then the earthe they treade upon: so as children neighbours and freindes (especially if they be poore) are rated the greatest burdens, which if things were right, would be the cheifest earthly blessings."

> The whole earthe is the Lordes garden: and he hathe given it to the sons of men to be tilld and improved by them: why then should we stand striving heere for places of habitation . . . and in the mene tyme suffer whole countrys as fruitfull and convenient for the use of man, to lye waste without any improvement?

Here and there in Winthrop's general consideration of the venture we can sense the weight of his personal predicament in his decision making. The profligate Henry—and Henry's financial demands—seem to have been in his mind when he wrote that "we are growne to that height of Intemperance in all excesse of Ryot, as no mans estate all most will suffice to keepe sayle with his equalls: and he that fayles in it, must live in scorn and contempt." Forth's departure from Cambridge—as well as the Arminian influence in the universities and the church at large—seem to have been in his mind when he noted that "the fountains of learning and Religion are so corrupted as . . . most Children, even the best wittes and of fayrest hopes, are perverted corrupted and utterly overthrowne." He was, however, more direct as he turned from a general consideration of the venture to the "Perticular Considerations" which he applied to himself. "My meanes heere," he wrote, "are so shortned (now my 3 eldest sonnes are come to age) as I shall not be able to continue in this place and imployment where I now am." He likened himself to a man wading through deep water. True, "there is required tallnesse, as well as Courage," but "if he findes it past his depth, and God open a gapp another waye, he may take it." The God who opened a way out of deep water did so only for a purpose, of course—that He might be served—an argument which allowed Winthrop both to resolve and justify the dilemma of retreating from a world which he was obliged to serve. "Which way the streame of Gods providence leades a man to the greatest good, he may, nay he must goe"; "if I should let passe this opportunitye, that talent which God hath bestowed on me for publike service, were like to be buried;" "I thinke I am the rather bounde to take the opportunitye for spendinge the small remainder of my tyme, to the best service of the Churche which I may."

Responses to Critics

Having stated his case generally, Winthrop turned to specific objections. Some might say, he wrote, that "to take awaye the good people" would be "a great wronge to our owne Churche and Countrye." But not so. Relatively few need go, and those few were not being fully utilized in the service of church and country as it was; their efforts were being devoted only to "theire owne private familys." More to the point, "since Christes tyme the Church is to be considered as universall, without distinction of countrys, so as he that dothe good in any one place serves the Church in all places." As for sending only the "yonge ones" and not "our best ministers and magistrates," Winthrop's answer was homespun and obvious: "It is a greater worke and requires more skillful artizans, to laye the foundation of a newe building, then to uphould or repaire one that is ready built."

Some might say, too, that our fears are exaggerated, Winthrop wrote, that "we have feared a Judgment a longe tyme, but yet we are safe." He had only to point to the Protestants of Rochelle and the Palatinate for answer: probably just such reasoning led them "to sitt still at home, and not look out for shelter. . . . The woefull spectacle of their ruine, may teache us more wisdome." But was it not tempting Providence to leave "a fruitfull lande" when "we may perishe by the waye or when we come there, either [by] hanginge hunger or the sworde"? This objection Winthrop brushed aside as savoring "to muche of the flesh" and trusting too little in the Lord. "If this course [of ours] be warrantable we must trust Gods providence for these thinges." As to the right of the emigrants to enter a land belonging to others, Winthrop first denied the Indians ownership—"That which is common to all is proper to none, these salvadge peoples ramble over muche lande without title or propertye"—then asserted the Indians' goodwill and the fact that "there is more than enough [land] for them and us." And he covered the whole question by again putting it in the context of a service to God, for the settlers would enter the Indians' land in order to bring them to a knowledge of God:

It is the revealed will of God, that the Gospell should be preached to all nations: and thoughe we knowe not, whither the Indians will receive it or not, yet it is a good worke, to observe Gods will in offering it to them.

At the Bury meeting and in the weeks and months following, Winthrop refined and amplified his notes. He sent copies to friends and acquaintances (with requests apparently that they pass the writings on to *their* friends and acquaintances). When a new pamphlet appeared—a laudatory description of New England's commodities sent from Salem by a minister who had gone over the year before—Winthrop had copies made and put into circulation. From some, Winthrop obtained the support and approbation he desired. From others, not. Margaret's brother was one who disapproved. "I can not but lament when I thinke of your journey," he wrote. He had talked to preacher Daniel Rogers of Wethersfield, and the good preacher, too, was "agaynst your goeing"; Rogers "would fayne meet with you, for your reasons doe not satisfie him."[6] To at least one critic Winthrop answered directly. Only a part of his letter—blunt and vehement—is extant (Document 9).[7] The critic was one of those who feared Winthrop was overly pessimistic about England's condition and overstated the imminence of God's retribution. By way of reply Winthrop pointed to the lamentations and prophecies of the Puritan preachers, rising to a furious crescendo in 1629:

> If our condition be good, why doe his Embassadours [the preachers], turne their messages into complaintes and threatninges? why doe they so constantly denounce wrathe and judgment against us? why doe they pray so muche for healinge if we be not sicke? why doe their soules wepe in secret? and will not be comforted, if there be yet hope that our hurt may be healed?

And in the clearest terms he reiterated the argument of the publicists: God had given man a general commandment to "encrease and multiply and replenish the earth and subdue it . . . that man may enjoye the fruit of the earth, and God may have his due glory from the Creature." Yet

> many of our people perish for want of sustenance and imployment, many others live miserably and not to the honor of so bountifull a housekeeper as the lord of heaven and earth is, through the scarcity of the fruites of the earth. the whole lande of the kingdom as it is reconed is scarce sufficient to give imployment to one half of the people.

The conclusion was obvious: "I will insist upon this one Argument. A lande overburdened with people, may ease it self, by sending a parte into some other Countryes which lye wast and not replenished." The vehemence reflects a traumatic dimension of the decision for America. About to wrench himself out of familiar ways, Winthrop desperately needed to be convinced by peer approval that he was right in going.

Notes

1. I follow the editors of Mass. Hist. Soc., *Winthrop Papers*, vol. II, pp. 106-11, on the authorship and dating of the various drafts of the documents discussed here—Winthrop's "Generall considerations for the plantation" and "Perticular Considerations in the Case of J:W:". For a contrary view see Frances Rose-Troup, *John White: The Patriarch of Dorchester and the Founder of Massachusetts* (New York: G.P. Putnam's Sons, 1930), chap. XIII who attributes authorship of the first to minister White.

2. Robert Reyce, *Suffolk in the XVIIth Century*, ed. Lord Francis Hervey (London: J. Murray, 1902), p. 2. Reyce was a near-neighbor of Winthrop's.

3. Michael Walzer, *The Revolution of the Saints* (Cambridge, Mass.: Harvard University Press, 1965) makes well the point of this disparate reaction.

4. See *e.g.*, Reyce's initial reaction to Winthrop's decision in a letter to Winthrop, August 12, 1629, Mass. Hist. Soc., *Winthrop Papers,* vol. II, pp. 105-6.

5. The following is drawn from the versions of the general and particular considerations in ibid., pp. 114-17, 125-26. [*See Part 2, Documents 7, 8.*]

6. Deane Tyndal to John Winthrop, October 23, 1629, ibid., pp. 162-63.

7. The fragment of this letter is printed in ibid., pp. 121-24. [*See Part 2, Document 9.*]

8

Governor Winthrop

In noting the "Perticular Considerations" which led him to decide for emigration, Winthrop's very first point was his own paramountcy with regard to the venture: "It is come to that issue, as, in all probabilitye, the wellfare of the plantation depends upon my assistance," he wrote, "for the maine pillers of it beinge gentlemen of highe qualitye, and eminent partes, ... are determined to sitt still, if I deserte them."[1] The assertion is surprising, even stunning. For among the gentlemen-emigrants, Winthrop's status—as even he implies—was not nearly so high as that of a Sir Richard Saltonstall, less even than that of Isaac Johnson. Moreover, Winthrop was certainly not among the first movers of the emigration. And his activities in regard to the New England project were, at the very most, merely peripheral until after his agreement to emigrate. Wherein lay his importance? Indeed, one might be tempted to write off his assertion as a bit of self-delusion if it were not for the fact of his very rapidly assuming a dominant position as the Massachusetts Bay Company carried through the transfer of government to the emigrants first broached by Craddock on July 28.

Craddock's July proposal, recall, had borne no immediate results, but conversations along the lines it laid down had clearly been continuing. In mutually agreeing to be prepared to sail in March 1630 (the agreement at Cambridge of August 26) the emigrating gentlemen stipulated one provision, that "the whole governement together with the Patent for the said plantacion bee first by an order of [the Company] legally transferred and established to remayne with us."[2] In effect, they went Craddock one better by requiring that the patent—the royal charter by which the king authorized the company to run its own affairs—physically accompany them to New England. Two days following the agreement, the company met in London to consider the proposition. Two committees were appointed, one to prepare arguments for the transfer, one to prepare arguments against, and on the next day, following the committee reports, the principle of a transfer was voted affirmatively.[3] However, problems remained. Such a transfer was unprecedented. Was it legal? How could the financial investment already made by those members of the company *not* emigrating be protected? By what means could the transfer be formally effected? These questions were raised at a meeting of the company on September 29 but were deferred "untill Sr. R. Saltonstall, Mr. Johnson, & other gentlemen bee come upp to London & may bee heere present."[4] Winthrop was one of the "other gentlemen" and was on hand in London by October 5. A hectic two weeks ensued. The "advice of learned councell" was solicited on the question of the legality of the transfer and they apparently advised as to its propriety. Complicated and lengthy negotiations gradually resolved the financial problems, with Winthrop clearly having a hand in these sometimes frustrating negotiations, writing Margaret on October 15 that he had spent "all this daye till 8: of the clocke this eveninge abroad about businesse, and yet have dispatched but litle."[5] (The company records of the same day record him for the first time as being present at its meeting.) The formal transfer of the government was finally effected in the simplest of fashions on October 20 by the election of new officers from among the emigrants, and physically transferring the charter to them. Winthrop, Saltonstall, Johnson and Humphrey were all nominated for the governorship, but the company members—"having received extraordinary great commendacions of Mr. John Winthrop, both for his integritie & sufficiencie"—gave a majority of their votes to him.[6] Modestly Winthrop conveyed the news to Margaret that same evening. It "hath pleased the Lorde to call me to a further trust in this businesse of the plantation, then either I expected or finde my selfe fitt for . . . . The onely thinge that I have comforte of in it is, that heerby I have assurance that my charge is of the Lorde and that he hath called me to this worke."[7]

Why Winthrop's paramountcy? Why his election to the governorship? It is a near complete conundrum. One possible explanation lies in the prior history of the Massachusetts Bay Company and its parent New England Company. In the first establishment of the company three primary groups were brought together: Dorchester men, Londoners, and Country gentlemen (including most prominently those about the household of the Earl of Lincoln). Among these groups there might well have been rivalries. Perhaps (and it can only be conjecture) the rivalries spilled over to the potential emigration. Perhaps the emigration itself, dominated as it was by the Country gentlemen, exacerbated an existent rivalry between the Country gentlemen and the Londoners, who were the most important of the investors remaining behind and who were seeking to protect their money. The extant materials offer only bare hints of such rivalries: the appointment of arbiters (attorney White and two clergymen) to determine differences between emigrants and stay-at-home investors; the nominations for the governorship, which can be interpreted as a London candidate (Saltonstall with his City ties), a Lincolnshire man (Johnson), a Dorchester candiate (Humphrey), and Winthrop; a stray line from an address Winthrop delivered to the investors in November 1629 in which he referred to "some jealousy at first."[8] In such a situation it is conceivable that Winthrop's paramountcy lay in that late entry into the affairs of New England which makes his importance surprising on the surface. With both London and Country ties, he was nevertheless unassociated in prior company affairs with any particular group.

Whatever the reason, however much his selection was the result of a fortuitous compromise, the company could not have done better in their choice. Winthrop appears to have blossomed as governor. As one scans his life to October 20 one discerns competence, true, but hesitancy and vacillation as well, and an ambivalence about his affairs—what is sought one day (his attorneyship, for example) is spurned the next. It was, of course, a product of his Puritanism—an exaggerated impetus to serve God by working assiduously at every wordly calling, yet forever to question the godliness of the call and ultimately deny, for God's sake, the rewards which working well in the world might bring. (Puritanism in his case was evoking a curious lassitude which historians hardly ever impute to it.) Vacillation, hesitancy, ambivalence, and lassitude disappeared with Winthrop's entrance into the governorship, however, to be replaced by their opposites. Again it was a product of his Puritanism: in Winthrop's way of thinking, God had clearly set him this task, hence the demands of God and worldly affairs were no longer in opposition.

Preparations for Departure

From his election on October 20 until late March 1630, when he boarded ship for the voyage, Winthrop was a flurry of activity. The very letter in which he informed Margaret of his election closed on a note of business: "Let John [Junior] enquire out 2: or 3: Carpenters: and knowe how many of our neighbours will goe, that we may provide shipps for them."[9] (In the end, some one hundred of the one thousand passengers of the Winthrop fleet would come from within ten miles of Groton.) Specialists in addition to carpenters had to be recruited: brickmakers, fishermen, semiprofessional soldiers to head up the settlement's defenses, and ministers to care for the spiritual life of the emigrants. In early November Winthrop and the other leaders met in London with an assemblage of preachers to obtain their advice as to appropriate clerics. Ordnance and ammunition had to be provided, and the leaders conferred with England's master gunner and the commander of the London artillery. John Junior was sent off to sketch harbor fortifications which might serve as models for those to be built in New England. (Along the way he spied a new type of windmill which he thought appropriate to "Corne milles saw miles etc.; . . . if there be made any use of it, I desire New England should reape the benefit," he wrote his father in reporting in detail on the invention.)[10] Ships had to be leased, and supplies had to be gathered for the voyage and the anticipated first hard year of settlement, everything from foodstuffs to cordage and cattle. And the conditions under which settlers (other than specialists provided by the company) would go had to be arranged; ultimately passage was set at five pounds sterling for each adult, somewhat less for children, and personal freight at four pounds a ton. The preparations and attendant publicity prompted groups to prepare for a New England voyage independent of Winthrop and the company—one group of 80 men, women, and children from England's West Country, another of 140 gathered in and around Dorchester under the auspices of the Reverend John White—and the relationship of these independents to the company had to be worked out. All the while Winthrop had his personal affairs to attend to, inventorying his English lands in preparation for their sale, establishing a fund which would care for Margaret and the younger children while he was gone, assembling his effects for the voyage—including a "sackcloth to pack your things in" for which he paid four shillings to one John Tolly.[11]

In all this flurry of activity little thought seems to have been given to the future, to what the settlers would build in New England. Stray bits and pieces indicate the physical form that Winthrop and the other leaders expected their settlement to assume: one central community within which each settler would have his house and garden; in the surrounding area "the fields which the generality would cultivate and on which they would graze their cattle, and the larger farms granted to the more wealthy and prominent as their due."[12] But no firm evidence exists to indicate that the leaders conferred about, let alone agreed upon, any concrete form which they would have either society in general or the churches in particular take[13] —an important omission in the light of the subsequent historiography of New England. Haste marked their departure, of course. The decision for America was precipitously made and executed—only a year elapsed between the closing of Parliament and their sailing. Perhaps there was no time for formal considerations which might have left a historical record, and planning for the future was a matter of quick, informal, unrecorded conversations.[14] Yet even during the enforced idleness of the two-month voyage to America aboard the *Arbella*, when Winthrop clearly turned his mind to the future and prepared a lay sermon for delivery to his fellow passengers—"A Modell of Christian Charity"—he could only express his hopes in vague terms (Document 10).[15]

The new society would be one of well-ordered degrees, for, as Winthrop wrote, "God Almightie in his most holy and wise providence hath so disposed of the Condicion of mankinde, as in all times some must be rich, some poore, some highe and eminent in power and dignitie; others meane and in subieccon." Responsibility and deference would bind each degree and each man to every other for the good of the whole, God ordering that "the riche and mighty should not eate upp the poore, nor the poore, and dispised rise upp against theire superiors," that "every man might have need of other, and from hence they might be all knitt more nearly in the Bond of brotherly affeccion." How in specific terms would this be accomplished? Winthrop offered no new and spectacular way to the social nirvana. Very simply:

> Whatsoever wee did or ought to have done when we lived in England, the same must wee doe and more allsoe where wee goe: That which the most in theire Churches maineteine as a truthe in profession onely, wee must bring into familiar and constant practise ... wee must love brotherly without dissimulation, wee must love one another with a pure hearte fervently wee must beare one anothers burthens, wee must not looke onely on our owne things, but allsoe on the things of our brethren. ... wee must delight in eache other, make others Condicions our owne rejoyce together, mourne together, labour, and suffer together, allwayes haveing before our eyes our Commission and Community in the worke, our Community as members of the same body.

The values expressed were those which the governor had imbibed at Country Groton, as exaggerated by the Puritan preachers to whom he listened.

Notes

1. Mass. Hist. Soc., *Winthrop Papers*, vol II, p. 125.
2. Ibid., p. 152.

3. The company's reasons for approving are not germane to Winthrop's decision. On one level, of course, the lay Puritans of the company would be sympathetic to the lay Puritans emigrating. On another level, however, the emigration of prominent gentlemen and those lesser souls who would follow them, at no expense to the company, represented an infusion of capital which the company sorely needed; the nonemigrating members need only insure a consideration of their prior investments—as they did—to hold open a possibility of a profit from this new capital.

4. Shurtleff, ed., *Records*, p. 52.

5. Mass. Hist. Soc., *Winthrop Papers*, vol. II, p. 159. See Frances Rose-Troup, *The Massachusetts Bay Company and Its Predecessors* (New York: The Grafton Press, 1930) for these negotiations.

6. Shurtleff, ed., *Records*, p. 59.

7. Mass. Hist. Soc.; *Winthrop Papers*, vol. II, p. 161.

8. Ibid., p. 176.

9. Ibid., p. 161.

10. Letter of January 18, 1629/30, ibid., pp. 193-94.

11. "Bill of John Tolly," February 13, 1629/30, ibid., p. 208.

12. Darrett B. Rutman, *Winthrop's Boston: Portrait of a Puritan Town, 1630-1649* (Chapel Hill, N.C.: University of North Carolina Press, 1965), p. 4.

13. There was speculation that the leaders of the emigration intended a particular and separate church, presumably along the lines of the English independent congregations in the Netherlands—"some scandalous misconceivings that runne abroade," according to one diarist (Mary Anne Everett Green, ed., *Diary of John Rous, Incumbent of Stanton Downham, Suffolk from 1625 to 1642* (["Camden Society Publications," 66; London, 1856], p. 54.) The leaders denied the rumors in *The Humble Request of His Majesties Loyall Subjects, the Governour and the Company Late Gone For New England; To the Rest of Their Brethren In and of the Church of England* (London: John Bellamie, 1630).

14. This is the implicit position of Perry Miller, *Orthodoxy in Massachusetts, 1630-1650* (Cambridge, Mass.: Harvard University Press, 1930), p. 122: "Into the activities of the Company itself during the crowded months before the migration we are permitted only a few tantalizing glimpses, and these not extensive enough to justify a positive declaration of the ecclesiastical sentiments entertained by the secular leaders. But most assuredly these men were busy at the time discussing what form the churches of the New World should assume." Cf. Rutman, *Winthrop's Boston*, Appendix II: "Were the Emigrants of 1630 'Non-Separating Congregationalists'?"

15. The "Modell" is printed in Mass. Hist. Soc., *Winthrop Papers*, vol. II, pp. 282-95. [*See Part 2, Document 10.*]

9

In New England

The New England in which Winthrop arrived in the summer of 1630 was a land where, as his son subsequently wrote, there were "all thinges to doe, as in the beginninge of the world."[1] A wilderness (in English eyes) had to be turned to cultivation. Homes, farm buildings, roads and bridges had to be built. Familiar institutions had to be reestablished. In this welter of activity, Winthrop held firm to the commitment—the calling—he had found when he made his decision for America. He had determined then that he had been set to the task of leading the emigration by God; he did not falter in this belief and until his death in 1649, in one position or another—most often as Massachusetts' governor—he served New England, and, through New England, God.

The life was not materially rewarding; indeed, at his death Winthrop was probably less well off than at his arrival. Neither was it without disappointments, even tragedy. Of the sons for whom he was so concerned in 1629, two died in 1630. Henry, having missed sailing on the *Arbella*, arrived on a subsequent ship, only to drown in a tidal creek within a matter of days. "My sonne Henry, my sonne Henrye, ah poore childe," the father wrote to Margaret.[2] Forth died suddenly in England before he could sail. But John Junior, arriving with Margaret and the remainder of the family in the summer of 1631, found his calling in America; ultimately he would become governor of Connecticut. So too did the younger children as they matured in New England. Others among the settlers might come to question (however faintly) their own decisions for America, as minister Thomas Shepard did: "I was tempted to fear that I had been out of my way in occasioning any to come to this wilderness."[3] But Winthrop never seems to have done so. He found fulfillment.

The fulfillment was personal, however, just as his decision for America had been personal. Yet on the basis of his decision much of a public nature was to be built. Winthrop, as we have seen, did not have a concrete plan for New England as he sailed in 1630, but a particular "New England Way" did in time evolve. The notion of a single centralized settlement disappeared in the immediate aftermath of the arrival; the settlers dispersed into clusters, and the New England town began its evolution. The exigencies of forming institutions where none existed forced hard decisions upon the leaders, particularly in the formation of churches for the towns. Laymen like Winthrop led in the early churches—only four ministers arrived with the Winthrop fleet—and the laymen made only rough and ready beginnings. But after 1633 the Puritan preachers began arriving in larger and larger numbers. By then, rising Arminianism had come to dominate the English hierarchy to a degree it had not done before, and Arminian bishops and archbishops began a policy of "thorough," seeking to enforce conformity by depriving Puritan preachers of their pulpits and lectureships. Pushed from old England by their deprivations, pulled to New England by the success of their lay followers who had gone earlier and a consequent promise of a freedom to preach which was being denied them in England, individual preachers made *their* decisions for America. They brought with them an authority and expertise in religious affairs, quickly assumed leading roles in the churches, and by their near-countless sermons exaggerated for New England as a whole the social ideals ("calling," for example) which we have already discerned in Winthrop. But they did more.

Seizing upon the laymen's rough beginnings in the churches, the preachers began honing a specific congregationalism for New England and justifying it theologically as God's one and true way. The sacraments of the church (baptism and communion) were made available only to church members, and membership was confined to those who could demonstrate by conduct and by professions of faith and grace that they were most probably among God's elect saints—this against the custom of England which held that church membership was national. The basis of a church was construed as a covenant—its would-be-members agreeing with each other and with God to be a church. Church authority was construed to lie in the membership (or congregation) of each church independently, each calling to its service whatever minister it pleased, for example, each disciplining its own membership, although the individual churches and their ministers were freely and voluntarily to cooperate to maintain a broad semblance of uniformity. Church and civil governments were in theory separated, although the civil governors were to be "nursing fathers" supporting orthodoxy in the church, while the advice of ministers in civil affairs was not to be eschewed. All this, again, was in contrast with England where church government lay in the hands of the hierarchy, and the king was the "supreme governor" of the church.

We need not elaborate here upon either the evolving New England Way in town and church or the effect of that way in the subsequent evolution of an American Way.[4] It is enough to say that a peculiar way *did* appear, and that fact had an almost immediate effect upon the way men viewed the motivations of 1629. The agonizing, personal decision for America that Winthrop made was forgotten; so, too, were the roots of that decision (his Country-Puritan alienation from the way of English life in general and his own life in particular), and the vagueness of his hopes for New England. The New England Way itself was transmuted into the motivation of the founders. In effect, it came to be said that they left old England with the intention of establishing that which ultimately evolved in New England. Edward Johnson, in the first formal history of New England (published in 1654) put the interpretation succinctly. To him the emigrants of 1629 were part of Christ's army, martially arrayed by a herald, led by their ministers, and given their commission by God himself, one commanding them to establish abroad a Congregational Way:

> Let the matter and forme of your Churches be such as were in the Primitive Times (before Antichrists Kingdome prevailed) plainly poynted out by Christ and his Apostles, in most of their Epistles, to be

> ... gathered together in Covenant of such a number as might ordinarily meete together in one place, and built of such living stones as outwardly appeare Saints by calling.[5]

At the same time the chronology of events was collapsed. Winthrop and his fellows had certainly felt ill-at-ease in England and fearful of the future, but they had not been persecuted. Persecution—if we would call it that—came in the 1630s when Arminianism peaked and embarked on thoroughness. This later persecution was pushed back to 1629, however, and exaggerated. Johnson again: Christ's army was composed of the "Oppressed, Imprisoned, and scurrilously derided."[6] Cotton Mather, writing his epochal *Magnalia Christi Americana* at the end of the seventeenth century, saw the emigration the same way. He was writing "the story of the folks thus 'driven into the wilderness,'" and while he "would relate it without all intemperate expressions of our anger against our drivers, before whom the people must needs go," nevertheless "it was a *PERSECUTION*; a *fury*."

> The persecuted servants of God, under the English Hierarchy, had been in *a sea of ice mingled with fire*; though the *fire* scalded them, yet such cakes of ice were over their heads, that there was no getting out; but the *ice* was now broken, by the American offers of a retreat for the pure worshippers of the Lord into a wilderness.[7]

The subsequent historiography of 1629 has largely emphasized these two points: a flight from persecution; a precise intent to establish a New England Way. Such simplification is a highly efficient tool in history for there is great explanatory power in simply asserting that men are forced to act as they do, or, alternatively, that men intend the results of their acts. (In the present case, of course, the explanatory power is doubled, for both assertions are made.) It ignores, however, the subtle interplay of mind and events by which men—Winthrop in this instance—come to their decisions, and the subtle interplay of countless individual decisions which sum to the human story.

Notes

1. John Winthrop, Jr., to Mr. Oldenburg, Secretary of the Royal Society, November 12, 1668, Mass. Hist. Soc., *Proceedings*, Series 1, vol. XVI (1879), pp. 236-37.

2. Letter of July 16, 1630, Mass. Hist. Soc., *Winthrop Papers*, vol. II, pp. 302.

3. Michael McGiffert, ed., *God's Plot: The Paradoxes of Puritan Piety, Being the ... Journal of Thomas Shepard* (Amherst, Mass.: University of Massachusetts Press, 1972), p. 106.

4. See among the author's other works *American Puritanism* and *Winthrop's Boston*; Morgan's *Puritan Dilemma*; and Hall's *Faithful Shepherd*, all cited *supra*.

5. *[Edward] Johnson's Wonder-Working Providence, 1628-1651*, ed. J. Franklin Jameson, (New York, C. Scribner's Sons, 1910), pp. 25-26.

6. Ibid., p. 24.

7. Cotton Mather, *Magnalia Christi Americana; or, The Ecclesiastical History of New-England*, vol. I (Hartford, S. Andrus and Son, 1852), pp. 65, 68.

part two

Documents of the Decision

The historian's mind is not a *tabula rasa* as he approaches the documents appropriate to his subject. He comes to them with the historiography of the subject in mind—suspicious that his predecessors have failed to tell the story rightly, yet at the same time broadly informed as to the general events of the time and place. (Admittedly the reader of this volume has not been provided with all of this historiographic preparation; a limited space allows only a sampling in Part Three. But the footnotes of Part One supply the titles of a few additional works, most notably those of contemporary scholars of English Puritanism and of pre-Civil War England—the latter suggesting the dichotomization between "Court" and "Country" of which so much is made.) He has in mind, too, a thought as to the way human behavior might be analyzed, in this case a situational approach which establishes two propositions: Winthrop's decision for America was a reaction to his definition of the situation surrounding him at the time of the decision; his definition of that situation was the product of a complex process of successive situational definitions and responses stringing back through his life to—where? childhood? the cradle? the womb? This second proposition might well lead some modern historians to attempt ex post facto psychoanalysis. But the documents would probably not sustain analysis at such a level. For us the proposition requires simply the acknowledgment that our study cannot be limited to the single decision of 1629, but must span as much of Winthrop's life as possible. The two propositions together give rise to a series of questions which both guide the search for documents and organize the documents we find. Winthrop's basic definition of himself and his world, that which gave meaning to the situations he would confront at and about the time he decided for America, would depend to a large extent upon the way he was educated to the world, the words and acts of parents, teachers, clergymen. Most of this is, of course, lost to us, but can we recover any of it? Documents 1 and 2 are suggestive. Is there anything of Winthrop's own production which might give evidence of this basic orientation? Winthrop's "Experiencia" (Document 3) and his participation in the preparation of the "Common Grevances Groaninge for Reformation" (Document 4) might serve. His correspondence (Documents 5-a through 5-i) brings us closer to the actual event in question and culminates in an indication of traumatic alienation (his letter to Margaret of May 15, 1629). Somewhere along the line an American alternative must have been offered Winthrop—this is implicit in his finally deciding for America. In what form? (Document 6.) Finally, how did Winthrop himself explain his decision, and how is the explanation—itself an act undertaken in the context of a situational definition—to be understood? (Documents 7 through 10.) The context of these documents has for the most part been set in the narrative of Part 1. Little need be added here. But as the critical reader proceeds he ought to be asking two related questions:

1. Does the narrative and interpretation of Part One violate any document in any way?

2. Do the documents suggest—as they well might to another eye—any other interpretation of Winthrop's decision for America?

1

The Social Order

Homilies were sermons prepared by a general convocation of the clergy of England and issued on the authority of the King's Council to be read periodically in all the churches of the realm. They tended to reflect generally accepted propositions—the pervasive mind-set of the time—rather than debatable points. The following is taken from "An Exhortation to Obedience" which first appeared in the mid-1500s and was generally reprinted through the mid-1600s.

Document†

Almighty god hath created & appointed all thynges in heaven, earth, & waters, in a most excellente & perfecte order. In heaven he hath appoynted distinct or several orders & States of Archangels & Angels. In earth he hath assigned & appointed kings, princes with other governors under them, all in good and necessary order. The water above is kept, and rayneth downe in due time and season. The sunne, moone, starres, rainebow, thunder, lightnyng, cloudes, and all byrdes of the ayre do kepe theyr order. The earth, trees, sedes, plantes, hearbes, corne, grasse, & all maner of beastes, kepe themselves in their order. All the partes of the whole yere, as winter, somer, monethes, nightes & daies, continue in their order. All kindes of fishe in the sea, rivers & waters, with all fountaines, springes, yea, the seas themselves kepe their comely course & order. And man him self also hath all his partes, both within & without, as soule, heart, mynde, memory, understanding, reason, speache, wyth al and synguler corporall members of hys bodye, in a profitable, necessarye, & pleasaunt order. Every degree of people in theyr vocation, callyng & office, hath appointed to theym theyr duetie and order. Some are in hyghe degree, some in lowe, some kynges, and prynces, some inferiours and subjects, pryestes, and laymen, maysters and servauntes, fathers and chyldren, husbandes and wyves, ryche and poore, and every one have nede of other.

†From: "An Exhortation, concernynge good order & obedience, to rulers and Majestrates," in *Certayne Sermons appointed by the Queenes Majestie, to be declared and read* (London, 1562).

2

The Puritan Preacher and the Doctrine of Calling

William Perkins (1558-1602) was one of the most widely read of the Puritan preachers; we know, from entries in Winthrop's "Experiencia," that he was familiar with Perkins's works. "Calling" was a concept common to Englishmen—it is implicit in Document 1—but the preachers (and Winthrop) stressed it.

Document†

A vocation or calling, is a certain kinde of life, ordained and imposed on man by God, for the common good. First of all I say, it is a *certaine condition or kinde of life:* that is, a certaine manner of leading our lives in this world. For example, the life of a king is to spend his time in the governing of his subjects, and that is his calling: and the life of a subject is to live in obedience to the Magistrate, and that is his calling. The state and condition of a Minister is, to leade his life in preaching of the Gospell and the word of God, and that is his calling. A master of a family, is to leade his life in the government of his family, and that is his calling, In a word, that particular and honest manner of conversation, whereunto every man is called and set apart, that is (I say) his calling.

Now in every calling we must consider two causes. First, the efficient and author thereof. Secondly, the final and proper end. The author of every calling, is God himselfe: and therefore Paul saith; *As God hath called every man, let him walke,* vers. 17. And for this cause, the order and manner of living in this world, is called a *Vocation;* because every man is to live as he is called of God. For looke as in the campe, the Generall appointeth to every man his place and standing; one place for the horse-man, & another for the foot-man, and to every particular souldier likewise, his office and standing, in which hee is to abide called against the enemie, and therein to live and die: even so it is in the humane societies: God is the Generall, appointing to every man his particular calling, and as it were his standing; and in that calling he assignes unto him his particular office; in performance whereof he is to live & die. And as in a campe, no souldier can depart his standing, without the leave

†From: William Perkins, *A Treatise of the Vocations, or Callings of men, with sorts and kinds of them, and the right use thereof,* in *The Workes of That Famous and Worthy Minister . . . Mr. William Perkins* (London: I. Legatt, 1612), vol. I, pp. 750-52.

of the Generall; no more may any man leave his calling, except he receive liberty from God. Againe, in a clocke, made by the arte and handy-worke of man, there be many wheeles, and every one hath his severall motion, some turne this way, some that way, some goe softly, some apace: and they are all ordered by the motion of the watch. Beholde here a notable resemblance of Gods speciall providence over mankinde, which is the watch of the great world, allotting to every man his motion and calling: and in that calling, his particular office and function. Therefore it is true that I say, that God himselfe is the author and beginning of callings.

This overthroweth the heathenish opinion of men, which thinke that the particular condition and state of man in this life comes by chance, or by the bare wil and pleasure of man himself. Secondly, by this which hath bin said, we learn, that many perswading themselves of their callings, have for all this, no calling at all. As for example, such as live by usury, by carding and dicing, by maintaining houses of gaming, by plaies, and such like: For God is the author of every lawfull calling: but these and such miserable courses of living, are either against the word of God, or else are not grounded thereupon. And therefore are no callings or vocations, but avocations from God and his waies.

Now as God is the author of every calling, so he hath two actions therein. First, he ordaineth the calling itself. And secondly, he imposeth it on man called: & therfore I say, *vocation is a certain kind of life, ordained & imposed by God.* For the first, God ordaineth a calling, when he prescribeth and commandeth the same, in, and by his word: and those callings and states of life, which have no warrant from Gods word, are unlawfull. Now God in his word, ordaineth callings two waies. First, by commanding and prescribing them particularly, as he doth the most weightie callings in the family, Church, or common-wealth. Secondly, by appointing and setting downe certaine lawes and commandements, generally; whereby we may easily gather, that he doth either approove, or not approove of them, though they bee not particularly prescribed in the word.

The second action of God, which is the Imposition of callings, is, when he doth particularly set apart any man, to any particular calling: and this must be understood of all callings in the world. Now God doth this two waies. First by himselfe immediately, without the helpe of any creature. Thus in the beginning was *Adam* called & appointed to dresse the garden of Eden. Thus *Abraham* was called from the idolatrie of his fore-fathers, and received into the covenant of grace. Thus was Moses called to bee a Prince over the Israelites, to guide them out of Egypt, into the promised land. And in the new Testament, thus were the Apostles called to preach the Gospel. Secondly, God cals mediately by meanes, which be of two sorts; men and angels. By an angel was Philip, being a Deacon, to be an Evangelist; and the sette or appointed callings in Church and common-wealth, are ordinarily disposed by men, who are in this matter the instruments of God. And therefore men lawfully called by them, are truely called of God. Thus the Elders of Ephesus, called by the Apostles and the rest of the Church, are said to be called by the holy Ghost. And thus we see how God is the author of every calling.

The finall cause or ende of every calling, I note in the last words of the description; *For the common good:* that is, for the benefite and good estate of mankinde. In mans body there be sundrie parts and members, and every one hath his severall use and office, which it performeth not for it selfe, but for the good of the whole bodie; as the office of the eye, is to see, of the eare to heare, and the foote to goe. Now all societies of men, are bodies; a family is a bodie, and so is every particular Church a bodie, and the common-wealth also: and in these bodies there be severall members, which are men walking in severall callings and offices, the execution whereof, must tend to the happy and good estate of the rest; yea of all men every where, as much as possible is. The common good of men stands in this, not only that they live, but that they live well, in righteousnes and holines, and consequently in true happinesse. And for the attainement hereunto, God hath ordained and disposed all callings, and in his providence designed the persons to beare them. Here then we must in generall know, that he abuseth his calling, whosoever he be that against the end thereof, imployes it for himselfe, seeking wholly his own, & not the common good. And that common saying, *Every man for himselfe, and God for us all,* is wicked, and is directly against the end of every calling or honest kinde of life.

Thus much of the description of *Vocation* in generall. Now before I come particularly to intreate of the speciall kinds of callings, there are two generall rules to bee learned of all, which belong to every calling.

The first: whatsoever any man enterprizeth or doth, either in word or deede, he must doe it by vertue of his calling, and he must keepe himselfe within the compasse, limits, or precincts thereof. This rule is laid downe in these wordes of the Apostle: *Let every man abide in that calling, wherein he was called:* the drift whereof is, to binde men to their callings, & to teach them to performe all their actions by warrant thereof. It is said, *Hebr.* 11.6. *Without faith it is impossible to please God: and whatsoever is not of faith, is sinne.* Whatsoever is not done within the compasse of a calling, is not of faith, because a man must first have some warrant and word of God to assure him of his calling, to do this or that thing, before he can do it in faith. . . . Contrariwise, when any man is without the compasse of his calling, hee is out of the way, and by this meanes he bereaves himselfe of the protection of the Almighty; and lies open and naked to all the punishments & plagues of God. . . . When Peter beyond the limits of his calling, would needes warme him at the high Priests fire, it cost him the breach of his conscience; for at the very voice of a Damosel he denied Christ with cursing and banning. And the Exorcists in the Acts, that without sufficient calling, tooke on them to conjure evill spirits in the name of Jesus, were overcome by the same spirits, and were faine to flie away naked & wounded. In a word, looke what judgements befall men, marke well the time and circumstance thereof, it shall be found, that they are cast upon them by the hand of God, when they are forth of their callings, which God hath prescribed them to keepe. Therefore this must alwaies be remembered and practised carefully; that we doe take nothing in hand, unlesse wee have first ranged our selves within the precincts of our callings.

The second generall rule which must bee remembred, is this: That *Every man must doe the duties of his calling with diligence:* and therefore Salomon saith, Eccl. 9:10. *Whatsoever is in thine hand to do, do it with al thy power.* S. Paul bids him that ruleth, rule with diligence; and every man to wait on his office, Rom. 12.8. And Jeremy saith, Jer. 48.10 *Cursed is he that doth the work of the Lord negligently.* That which Christ saith of the worke of our redemption, *It is meate and drinke for me to do my Fathers will,* the same must every man say in like sort of his particular calling. Of this diligence there be two reasons: first of all, the end why God bestowes his gifts upon us, is, that they might be imployed in his service, and to his glorie, and that in this life. Therefore Paul saith, *Redeeme the time:* and Christ, *Walke while ye have light.* And againe, *I must do his work while it is day:* For we see tradesmen and travellers rise early to their businesse, lest night overtake them. Secondly, to them which imploy their gifts, more is given, and from them which imploy them not, is taken that which they have: and labour in a calling is as pretious as gold or silver. Hereupon he that maimes a man, and disables him to do the worke of his calling, by Gods law is bound to give him the value of his labour, *Exod.* 21.19. And to like purpose our people have a common saying, that an occupation is as good as land, because land may be lost; but skill and labour in a good occupation is profitable to the end, because it will helpe at neede, when land and all things faile. And on the other side, we must take heede of two damnable sinnes that are contrary to this diligence. The first is idlenesse, whereby the duties of our callings, and the occasions of glorifying God, are neglected or omitted. The second is slouthfulnes, whereby they are performed slackly and carelessely. God in the Parable of the husband-man, cals them that are idle into his vineyard, saying, *Why stand ye idle all the day? Mat.* 20.6. And the servant that had received but one talent, is called an evill servant, because he was slouthfull in the use of it: for so it is said, *Thou evill servant and slouthful,* Mat. 25.26. S. Paul gives this rule to the Thessalonians, *Hee that will not labour, must not eate:* yet such a one he would have to bee noted by a letter, as walked inordinately. And by this he sheweth, that slouth and negligence in the duties of our callings, are a disorder against that comly order which God hath set in the societies of mankinde, both in church and common-wealth. And indeed, idlenes and slouth are the causes of many damnable sins. The idle body, and the idle braine, is the shop of the divell. The sea, if it mooved not, could not but putrifie: and the body, if it be not Stirred and mooved, breedeth diseases. Now the idle and slouthful person is a sea of corruption; and when he is most idle, Satan is least idle; for then is he most busie to draw him to manifold sinnes.

3

The Puritan and the World

During much of his life in England, Winthrop kept a journal of his religious "Experiencia," sporadically entering his temptations, occasionally moralizing to himself. Not meant to be read by others, the "Experiencia" seems as close as we can come to the private man. The following excerpts were entered in late 1616 and early 1617.

Document†

The fleshe is eagerly inclined to pride, and wantonnesse, by which it playes the tirant over the poore soule, makinge it a verye slave; the workes of our callings beinge diligently followed, are a speciall meanes to tame it, and so is temperance in diet, for idlenesse (under which are all suche workes as are doone to fullfill the will of the fleshe rather then of the spirit,) and gluttonie are the 2 maine pillars of the fleshe hir kingdome. See Eccl: I:13.

After I had somewhat shaked off my afliction, and had held in to a temperate course, and had been pretily wayned from the worlde, and had brought under my rebellious fleshe, and pretylye tamed it by moderate and spare diet, and houldinge it somewhat close to its taske, by prayer, readinge, meditation and the workes of my callinge, not suffering it to be idle nor yet to be busied in suche things as it did desire, etc: after a monthe or 5 weeks continuance thus, this wilye fleshe beganne to fainte, and seemed as thoughe it could not longe hould out, it grewe aguishe and lumpishe, etc: so as if Christ had not heere holpen me, I had through too light beleefe, and foolish pittie, lightened it of the burthen and letten it have more libertie to mine owne overthrowe; but God being mercifull to me, forced me (even against my will) to lay more loade upon it, and to sett it a greater taske, for he lett in suche discomforts, of anguish, feare, unquietnesse, etc. upon my soule, as made me forgett the grones of the fleshe and take care to helpe my pore soule, and so was the fleshe forced to be more stronge and lively, when it was putt to greater labour; yet as soone as the soule was at quiet againe, the fleshe fell to his former course, and grewe exceedinge discontented, when it remembered the fleshe potts of Egypt, the former pleasure, ease, recreations, mirthe, etc: which it had wont to enjoye. . . .

Jany 20 [1617]. Our [Court] Sessions were, against which (fearinge greatly mine owne frailtie) I did prepare myself by earnest prayer etc: and my

†From: Massachusetts Historical Society, *Winthrop Papers* (Boston, 1929-47), vol. I, pp. 193-96, 212-13, 215. Reprinted by permission of the Society.

tyme, as I rode, I spent as well as I could in good meditations, and kept my course of prayer etc: as well as conveniently I could while I was there, refraininge my mouthe, eyes, and eares from vanitie, as well as I could, and so it pleased God that I brought home my peace and good conscience with me, yet my love of goodness some what abated, which I perceived not till a daye or 2 after, when I began to be somewhat loathe to prayer and good communication; the fleshe beginninge to favoure itselfe, but it pleased God by prayer to quicken me againe. When I was at Sessions I kept a continuall watche (as neere as I could), but yet when I sawe and heard the great accompt and estimation that the wisdome, glorye, wealthe, pleasure and such like worldly felicitie was in with all, methought I hearde all men tellinge me I was a foole, to sett so light by honour, credite, welthe, jollitie etc: which I sawe so many wise men so much affecte and joye in, and to tye my comforte to a conversation in heaven, which was no where to be seene, no way regarded, which would bring my selfe and all my gifts into contempt, etc: These and the like baites did Sathan laye for me, and with these enymies he did ofte tymes sore shake my faithe; but Christ was in me, and uphelde my resolution, and he will uphould it (I truste and praye) that my faithe shall never faile. O Lord keepe me that I be not discouraged, neither thinke the more meanly of the portion which I have chosen, even to walke with thee, and to keepe thy Commandments, because the wise ones of this world doe not regarde but contemne these things. Thou assurest my heart that I am in a right course, even the narrowe waye that leads to heaven: Thou tellest me, and all experience tells me, that in this way there is least companie, and that those which doe walke openly in this way shalbe despised, pointed at, hated of the world, made a byworde, reviled, slandered, rebuked, made a gazinge stocke, called puritans, nice fooles, hipocrites, hair-brainde fellowes, rashe, indiscreet, vain-glorious, and all that naught is; yet all this is nothinge to that which many of thine excellent servants have been tried with, neither shall they lessen the glorie thou hast prepared for us. Teache me, O Lord to putt my trust in thee, then shall I be like mount Sion that cannot be removed. Amen.

Feb: 3. I went towards London, and returned soone, the 11. I went forthe sickly, but returned (I prayse God) safe, and healthie. Whereas I was wont to lose all my tyme in my journies, my eyes runninge upon everye object, and my thoughts varieing with everye occasion, it pleased God that I nowe made great use of my tyme, bothe in prayeing, singing, and meditatinge with good intention and muche comforte. Amongst other things, I had a very sweet meditation of the presence and power of the Holy Ghost in the hearts of the faithfull, howe he reveales the love of God in our hearts, and causeth us to love God againe; howe he unites all the faithfull in deed and in affection: howe he opens our understandings in the misteries of the gospell, and makes us to beleeve and obeye: and of the sweet consent betweene the worde and the spirit, the spirit leadinge and directinge us in all things according to the worde: I am not able to expresse the understandinge which God gave me in this heavenly matter, neither the joye that I had in the apprehension thereof. . . .

Feb. I kept on my course but yet up and downe, for the fleshe still gathered to itselfe, and sought its owne ease, pleasure, glorye, etc, and my heart grewe towards the worlde againe, so as the sweet relishe and estimation of Christ and salvation was even gone, untill God againe opened mine eyes to see my carnal affections, my slouthfulnesse, vanitye of minde, pride, falseheartednesse, infidelitye; no love to him in Christ, nor love to his saintes; my too muche account and estimation of the worlde, too busylye imployinge my thoughts in caringe for and delightinge in earthly things: so as I am thoroughly persuaded that the love of the worlde even in a smale measure, will coole, if not kill, the life of sinceritye in Religion, and will abolishe the verye memorye of heavenly affections: O Lord, crucifie the world unto me, that though I cannot avoyd to live amonge the baites and snares of it, yet it may be so truely dead unto me and I unto it, as I may no otherwise love, use, or delight in any the most pleasant, profitable, etc, earthly comforts of this life, then I doe the ayre which I continually drawe in, or the earthe which I ever tread upon, or the skye which I ever behould. O why should I doate with greater affection on other thinges which are of lesse use? . . .

Upon searche of my heart, and the sight of my secret sinnes and corruptions which still prevayled against me, I grewe into much feare, discomfort, and heavynesse. I was without joye; in God I could finde none, (I seemed so unworthye); In worldly things I durst take none (althoughe the devill did make me continuall and large offers,) but resolved with myselfe rather to continue in my perplexed estate then to have helpe by any other meanes then from the Lorde; so I prayed earnestly and gave my selfe to waite with patience, and in due tyme I found, accordinge to that of the Prophet Esaye 30. 15., in quietnesse and confidence was my strength. . . .

Havinge been longe wearied with discontent for want of suche employment as I could find comfort and peace in, I founde at last that the conscionable and constant teachinge of my familye was a speciall businesse, wherein I might please God, and greatly further their and mine own salvation, which might be as sufficient incouragement to my studye and labour therein as if I were to teache a publick Congregation; for as to the pleasing of God it was all one, and I perceived that my exercise therein did stirre up in me many considerations and much life of affection, which otherwise I should not so often meet with; so as I purpose by Gods assistance, to take it as a chiefe part of my callinge, and to intende it accordingly. . . .

I founde my heart, upon this meditation, willinge to sett upon any dutye, whilest I behelde my warrant in Gods book: and whereas sometymes many things did discourage me from dutye, as the judgment of the greatest parte, the unlikelynesse of successe, the evill acceptation of others, the feare of losse, disgrace, health, etc. now I remembred what Christ sayed, "Woe to the world because of offences, and blessed are they that shall not be offended in me": I perceived that these and suche like rubbes to our faithe were the offences that Christ doth partlye meane there, and I see that they that will take offence from the opinion of others, their owne corrupt reason, common experience, etc, shall never enjoye the comforte of livinge by faithe, for the

Childe of God must breake throughe all these and saye with Paul, Rom: [3.4.] Let God be true and every man a liar. O Lord I have sinned in that I have not beleeved thy worde that I might sanctifie thy name before thy people, but by thy grace I shall not dare heerafter once to doubt of thy holy and eternall truethe: Let it be sufficient encouragement and warrant to me in any thinge, that is thy Commandment, thy promise etc.

Resist the Devill and he will flee from you: this have I found true by ofte experience, for whereas upon the Sabbaothe and in hearinge of the worde etc, my heart would be most pestered with worldly thoughts, etc, so as I should have stronge desires to be thinkinge of some suche things at those tymes, which at other tymes I should not regarde; and from these snares I could not free myselfe, until it pleased the Lord, in prayer, to discover unto me that it was Satan that did thus followe me with his assaults; whereupon I sett myselfe against him by applyinge such places of scripture, as did best oppose his temptations: and thus doeinge, I have ofte tymes had my heart set at libertye from suche worldly thoughts and other his snares: The Lorde be praysed forever.

"Common Grevances Groaninge for Reformation"

It is presumed that the list of "Common Grevances" found among Winthrop's papers was prepared by Winthrop and several other Suffolk gentlemen for presentation to the Parliament of 1624 or to a Committee of its House of Commons. There were twenty-three grievances in all; sixteen are reprinted here.

Document†
Grevance. The Daylye Encrease of the Multitudes of Papistes
Remedye. It is desired that all papistes may be excommunicated in theire parrish churches every 6 monthes, and upon there not conformitie, the Significavit to be sewed out against them. And that some fundamentall lawe may be made for to remove all theire Children from them, to be trained up in the truth and syncerity of Religion at theire owne charges.
Motives.
1. They carye such wicked myndes to the State, that thar all wayes in study and action howe to betray yt and theire naturall Soveraigne into the handes of forreigne power, the greatest adversary which our Land hath.
2. This wilbe a great meanes to provide for defence of Religion and the safty of our Land.
3. Yt will in short tyme much decrease theire nombers, whoe now by our long sufferinge are much emboldened and dayly encoraged by the protection and mayntenance of forreigne partes.
Grevance. The Removeall of Indightementes.
Remedye. That noe Indightmente may be removed owte of the Countye or Courte where they were found, without a full consente of the Court or Sessions, but that they may be confessed, fyned or traversed in that Court or place where yt was first fownd and presented.

†From: Massachusetts Historical Society, *Winthrop Papers* (Boston, 1929-47), vol. I, pp. 295-308. Reprinted by permission of the Society.

Grevance. Abuse Aboute Presentementes and Commutation of Penance.

Remedye. That in all presentmentes into the Ecclesiasticall Courtes for matters of cryme as adultery, whoredome Inceste and such lyke, none shalbe admytted to purgation without lettres proclamatory sent 15 dayes before the Court unto the minyster and parish from whence the presentment came. And that noe commutation of pennance for any offence whatsoever, may be without the consent of the mynister and parrish where the fact befell, and that one third parte of the penance comuted may goe to thuse of the poore of the parish, as in settyng forth poore mens children to service and to be apprentices. . . .

Grevance. The Common Scarcitie of Woode and Tymber in most places of this Realme, increased by the small preservation of the owners, whoe are discoraged to mayntaine and provoked to fell by the unrewlines of the poorer sort, whoe doe from tyme to tyme by day and night make all havoke and wast of any thing that is cherished and preserved.

Remedye.

1. Noe owner or Farmor that shall fell any tymber tree or Bowlyng, for his owne buildinges or reparacons but to plant 2 trees for every one that he felleth and to be carefully preserved for 7 yeares after, And whosoever shall fell any tymber trees or Bowlinge to sell, to plant 3 trees for every one that he felleth:

2. None to stubbe up any grownd wood to the vallewe of one acre or more, without the consent of the 2 next Justices of peace, who haveing a commission sewed owt by the owner of the wood shalbe authorised by the oath of 12 men to enquire what damage yt shalbe to the Commonwealth, upon the retorne of which commyssion yt shalbe eyther allowed or disalowed.

3. Whosoever shall lopp or cobb, any trees or tymber trees or otherwise shall cut any grownd wood or any quicke, or severall spring in any hedges, or shall breake up or carry away any sortes of gates, Stiles, Bridges, leane trees, payles postes, rayles, hedges or any yong planted trees, shall lie in the howse of Correction and under the orders of the howse, untill the next Justice doe remytte him.

4. Whosoever shall sell any stollen woode or offer yt to be sold shalbe whipped in the next markett.

5. Whosoever shall buy any stollen wood shall likewise be whipped in open markett and pay treble the vallewe thereof to thuse of the poore of the howse of correction.

Grevance. The Extraordinary Casualties and Divastation by Fyers.

Motives.

1. The exceedeing ruine of buildinges, wherein consisteth the ma[jes]tie of kingdomes.

2. The earth the first parent of all materialls waxeth aged and barren in produceing her wonted supplie for such defectes.

3. This declineing age stirreth up all sortes to frugalitie and parsimonye.

4. The multitude of persons overthrowne by this meanes occasioninge a multiplicitie of patentes for ayde and releife: wherein albeit the commendable collection which is raysed toward releafe of fellowe feeleing necessity be greate: yet what with deputie collectors apparitors and Registers not halfe cometh to the patentes handes.
5. He that sawe his neighbours misery yesterday hath cause to feare his owne to day.
6. This accidente befalleing whiles every one owte of a tender affection is more ready to bewayle, then by stody of good meanes to prevent, rather taketh harte to encrease, then cause to abate.
7. The ground of such great losses, ar, untrustines of recles servantes, heedeles dames, careles maisters, and a supine negligence in all sortes, which after the greatest mishapps goe away unponished or unreproved: whereas yt weere more safely that every one shold be tyed to looke more warely to soe common an adversary.

Remedye. Soe sone as any fier befalleth, the next Justice of the peace shall presently send for the master of the howse to take recognisance of him or his sufficient dupitie for apparance at next quarter sessions, where the matter may be duly examined how the fier beganne wherein if yt shall appeare that the servant haveing all convenient tyme with all fytt matter and meanes for the dispatch of the busines intended, and yett was careles and negligent, the Court to commyt the servant to the howse of correction for 2 months etc.

But if the maisters be found guiltie, whoe through a gredines to dispatch much woorke with litle helpe at unseasonable tyms in the night seazon, or in tempestious wyndy weather doe sett theire servantes or children voyde of yeeres and discretion about workes above their reach and understandeyng, often tymes haveing noe fitt meanes or place, and soe oftentymes, wholl howses, streetes and parishes are burned, because that he was negligent of his owne good, is presumed may be recles of the common good, shall at the discretion of the Court be fyned and condemned to pay at the least the summe of v *li.* to the treasorer of the Kynges bench and marthialsey for that divysion, or else to be commytted unto the Gayle untill etc.

But yf the party ruynated and burned be soe heerby decayd as he is not able to satisfie the sentence delivered, because to ad affliction to affliction, ys not fyttyng for a Christian, and the law aymeth at the common good of every one in generall, rather then at any particular use sole, then the Court is to fyne him at theire discretion soe as the fyne or censure, be not soe litle as that it doth occasion a contempte of lawe and magistracie.

All pilferers and robbers in the tymes of fires and such casualties are to be ponished more severely and without all benefitt of their clergie. . . .

Grevance. The Decay of the Aunciente Trade of Sadlers
Motive.
1. The awncient mistery and company of Sadlers both in London and elsewhere throug owte this Realme who somtymes lived well

mayntained their familyes, payd Subsedies and all commonwelth charges, cannot sell their wares as in former tymes but are wholly decayd and impoverished, and soe utterly discoraged in their misteries by reason of the multitude of Coaches and Caroches used in every place, wherby our principall leather wherein we excell all other Contries is wasted and the prices of Bootes and Shoes is much emproved.

2. This equipage of Charrets, Coaches and Caroches was anciently the furniture ensignes ornamentes and honorable privelidges of Emperors Kinges great princes, nobles and other greate worthies, whoe defended the Contry by dynte of sword, and ever helped to mayntaine the Commonwelth in peace. But now are usurped by persons of meane respect quallitie and condicon, whoe never keepe hospitalitie in the places where they resyde, much lesse are they in Subsedy of the least vallewe, by reason whereof the safety of passengers in streetes and high wayes is much disturbed and indaungered.

Remedye. None under the degree of a Baron or Barons children, other then he that hath borne office in the Commonwelth in place of Judicature, as Justices and Judges in any of the Kinges Majesties Courts at Westm[inst]er or other then he that hath byn imployd in forreigne Ambassage, or that hath had the goverment of materiall regimentes, shall have use keepe or mayntaine for his owne use and behoofe any Charriot Coach or Caroch, unlesse he be valued in the Kinges Subsedy booke xx *li.* lande at the least and unles at the last muster he shewed and found 2 demy lawnces furnished for defence of the Realme, upon paine that every one soe offendeing contrary to this presente act to forfeit the summe of c *li.* of lawfull mony of England the one halfe to be payd to thuse of the Kinge, the other moyety to the party that shall sewe for the same.

Grevance. The Patentes for Collections Called Breefes

Remedie. That every Contry might releive theire owne poore and yf the towne be not able, that the Justices might take order at the quarter Sessions to releeve them out of the Tresury of the Kinges bench and martialsey and soe often as yt shall appear by an account that the tresury hath not sufficient, then the Justices to have power to rayse yt upon the Contry.

Motives.

1. Breifes collected on the Saboth doe much disturbe the devine service and the worshipp of God.

2. The Kinge and his subjectes are much abused, sometymes by false pattentes sometymes by false certificates: the losse being not one quarter thereof, yea often men pretende losses.

3. None soe fitt to releeve the poore as the County which may easilie enquire of the certyentie of the losse of the poverty and lyfe of the partie whither fitt to be releeved.

4. They have tyred the Church wardens, and of late hath much disquieted the hie Constables, they have cutt the throate of charitie amongst all men, litle is given and of that litle soe much to the Breefe farmors

Commissary Courtes and other that make Collections, that litle commeth to the pattenties.

Grevance. Scandalous and Dombe Ministers

Motives.

1. It is a grevous sinne against god and speaketh heavy to this nation that hath suffered yt all this while.
2. The want of ponishing of them is a g[rea]t emboldening of them and one especiall cause of the increase of popery and all other wickednes, and of the nomber of them.
3. They doe much harme by theire example, murthering many thousand sowles, which is a crying sinne.
4. There are many godly and painefull ministers which doe want Benefices and are keept owt by these and now would be much encoraged.

Reformation. That all dombe ministers might within 6 monthes after this present Session of parliamente be removed, and their benefices (if any) may be geven by the patrons to some other godly Learned and paynefull minister. . . .

Grevance. The Greate Delayes in Sewtes of Lawe.

Remedie. It is desired that noe sute may be prolonged above 4 tearmes and four Court dayes in the civell lawe, or that some other speedy course may be taken for expedition.

Motives.

1. It will ease the subject of greate charge and troble, whoe now have many long journies and spend much money.
2. In this length of Sewtes the playntife or defendante often dieth before the Sewte be ended, and then they must beginne againe.

Grevance. Pluralitie of Benefices.

Remedie. It is intreated that none might have but one Benefice and that whosoever now hath 2 or more, and doe not within 6 monthes after this present Session of parliament resigne all but one into the patrons handes they shalbe voyd *ipso facto.*

Motives.

1. It is a greate wrong to many parishes, for usually the curate preacheth not or else is very scandalous.
2. It keepeth many men of deserte and learning, and fitt to instructe, from employment or at the least from convenient maintenance.
3. It much discorageth parentes in bringing up theire children in learning seing it is soe hard to gett benefices and one man to have many and others none.
4. It is a greate Injustice that one man should take the paine and another goeing away with the gaine often tymes takeing 100 for 10 which is intollerable usury.

Grevance. The Ponishinge the Subject for Goeing to Another Parrish to Heare a Sermon When There is None in There Owne Parrish.

Remedie. It is desired none may be ponished for this godly facte eyther by the statute of I Elizab. 2: or by any ecclesiasticall courte.

Motives.

1. It will tend much to the glory of God and spreadeing of the Gospell, for many shall and will heare sermons, which now sitt at home and dare not goe.
2. It will stay many uncomfortable sewtes betwixt the parrishoners, and other ministers that preach not.
3. It will ease the subject of much troble, for many bad minded people (not thinkeing the want of a Sermon at home to be a reasonable lett to leave their owne parish which sayd lett the statute alloweth) doe take occasion by Justices and ecclesiasticall courtes to ponish and often to doe pennance for the leaveing of the ministers in the after none when he preacheth not. . . .

Grevance. The Suspension and Silenceing of Many Painfull Learned Ministers For Not Conformitie in Some Poynts of Ceremonies and Refuseing Subscription Directed by the Late Canons.

Remedie. It is much desired that such deprived suspended and silenced ministers may, by licence or permission of the Reverend fathers the Bishops in theire severall Diocesses instruct and preach unto the people in such places and parishes, where they may be imployed soe long as they shalbe ready to performe that legall subscription appointed by the statute of 13 Elizab: and employ themselves in theire minystery to holsome doctrine and exhortacon, live peaceably and quietly in their calling and shall not by writeing or preacheing impugne thinges established by publike auct[horit]ie.

Motives.

1. It hath not onely tended to the greefe of many loyall subjectes, but to the greate increase of popery and all other wickednes.
2. Scandalous and idle ministers have often byn set in their places, whereby many parishes have wanted instruction and have lyen more open to be seduced by yll affected people.
3. It hath removed many from their benifices which was theire freehold and debarred them of all meanes and maintenance for themselves wife and children.
4. These ministers weere very diligent and painefull in the worke of the ministery, with much frute and blessinge one theire labours.
5. These ceremonyes ar by our ch[urch] of England holden to be but thinges indifferent, and noe parte of godes worshipp, and therefore the lesse cause that they should be soe severely urged upon the conscience of men especially as they are in somme Diocesses, where (to the overthrow of many a lecture) noe minister at home nor abrode, Sabboth day or weeke day at any Lecture, Baptisinge, Buriall or mariadge may preach but he must first weare the Surplisse and reade prayers, and though he cometh 12 mile of that mornynge.

Grevance. The Pittifull Complainte of the Orphanes Fatherlesse and Many Poore Creditors When the Father Dieth Intestate, or Makinge a Will, the Executors Refuse Leaveinge Behinde But Litle Moveables but Greate Yerely Revenues, the Heyre Goeth Away With All the Lands, Debts Be Unpayed Children Not Educated Nor Porcions Provided for Them.

Remedie. It is desired some order may be taken that within 6 months after any such partie shall thus die for the sale of some landes or geveing of somme yeerely porcions out of the landes for the speedy paym[en]te of debtes reysing of portions and mayntenaunce to thuse of the children.

Motives.

1. It undoeth many poore creditors overthroweth many a childe for want of maintynance and porcion, and often forceth the yonger brother to desperate courses.

2. It is often much against the minde and will of the deceassede wanteing time to make his will.

3. It breedeth often tymes much strife and contention betwixt the elder brother and the rest of the children.

4. It is against all equitie that one should be a gentelman to have all, and the rest as beggers to have nothinge. . . .

Grevance. Ministers Who Have Cure of Sowles Doe Practise Phisicke For Gaine.

Motives.

1. By how much the sowle is more precious then the body: by soe much the more owght it always to be regarded and esteemed.

2. Yf the best Sheepeherdes that ever weere, found them selves wanteing in tyme and store for food and provision for there flock, then how canne he well, or with any comforte feede his flock, that taketh up every weeke 5 dayes for theire bodyes and but one for their sowles.

3. If experience teacheth that God never blessed any whoe forsooke and neglected this their vocation being the first that ever was, and unto which with soe solemne a voice they have consecrated themselves then how doe they looke to prosper in this world, or to escape at the latter day that heavy reckoninge which they are to make, for usurping of an other function to the manefest neglect of that greate charge of soe many precious sowles commytted to theire oversight.

Remedie. That none whoe hath consecrated himselfe to the office of the minystery, and hath accepted of a pastorall charge with care of sowles, shall there withall professe and practise Phisike for any gaine or the smalest lucre what soever upon paine to be deprived *ipso facto* of all his ecclesiasticall promotions.

Grevance. The Greate Decay of Feasants and Patriges With an Exceding Disorder in Haukeinge.

Motive.

1. The exercise of haukeing hath byn alwayes a peculiar disporte of Regallitie, nobilitie, and gentilitie.

2. What soever the earth bringeth forth in any place more excellent, the Subject owte of a necessary dutye to his Superior, owght to reserve the same to thuse of his Soveraigne, as a parte of that owtward and proper ornam[en]te of his high ma[jes]tye and dignitie.

3. The difference betwene principalitie and popularie that alwaies have byn such, that from the lawe of nature order and antiquitie, a

perpetuall precedencie and dominacion hath byn in the one and an invyolable law of conformitie and submission hath byn in thother.

4. Supreame magistrates and nobles ever toyling at the helme of the Commonwelth and all wayes watching for the preservacion of the same, to geve a refresheing delight and a new vigor of Spirit to theire wearied bodyes have a royall prerogative in the best recreations and delightes unfytting for inferior populare.

5. Many of the very meane sort and condicion whoe have presumed of this generous skill of falkenry, and from the variety of hawkes which they doe keepe, doe adventure upone the contrye nere adjoyneing to give exercise to theire Ostreges, whereby the wonted store of game, which was wont liberally to furnish both prince noble and gentle is now spoyled and destroyed.

6. It hath byn fownd that one skarce a gentelman of the first exemplicacion doth keepe in his howse at one tyme 4 caste of haukes enough to ravyne the store of a large circuit and contry as there eagernes and immoderacy in those sportes sheweth, when store of game falleth owt, that by Michell the store of that yeere is spent and gone.

7. Many under the pretence of haukeinge doe in the day tyme range over large circuitts to spie owte what covies and hauntes ech place affordeth and in the night followeing or very soone after with nettes and such like engines doe take them.

8. Many handycraftes men in good townes and otherwise doe in the night tyme, with nettes doges and engines take what soever they can spie owte in the day whereby the game is utterly spoyled.

Remedie. To reduce this generous exercise of hawkeinge to be used onely by the nobilitie gentilitie and better sorte of ample possessions and revennues.

1. None to keepe any hawke or hawkes under the title or degree of an esquire, or beinge in the subsedy xx *li.* lande, or whoe haveing landes of his owne wherein to hawke, excepted to every owner such breed of hawkes which shall tymber and eyre within any of his woodes and precinctes.

2. None at one tyme to maintaine one caste of hawkes for his sporte not comprehendinge therein any Sparhawke merlowe or Hobbie but he shalbe charged to finde at the next muster one demy lawnce furnished and for 2 castes of hawkes 2 lawnces furnished.

3. If any person of abilitie qualified by former statutes to keepe any nettes and engines to take any feasauntes and patriges in the day time be duly convicted to have taken any in the night by himselfe or by his deputye shall besides his forfeyture in the former statutes mencioned loose all his right or qualification for 7 yeeres after to take any in the day with any hawke engine or nett.

4. Every one that shall keepe in his howse any net and engine to take feasantes and patriches haveinge noe quantitie of ground in his owne occupienge nor otherwise qualified accordinge to the Statutes to forfeyt v *li.*, or to be whipped in the next markett.

5. Every Barbor who doth make nettes and engines shall yeerely before the feast of Michell yeilde up a trewe certificate in writeing unto the next 2 Justices of the peace what nettes for partriges or faysayntes, he hath mended, made, lent or sold, to whom and to what persons, upon paine to answeere this contempte the Sessions followeinge. . . .

Grevance. The Subjects of This Kingdome are Oppressed by Chargeable Suits, and Their Bodyes Arrested and Imprisoned for Every Smale Debt and Trespas to the Undoeinge of Many Poore Familyes and to the Great Damage of the Com[mon] w[eal]th.

This comes partly by reason of the multitude of Atturnies in the Courtes at West[minster] and partly through the pride and malice of the com: people, and partly through the multitude and lewdnesse of Baylyfs.

Many Atturneyes (abusing their priveledges) will take out processe against their neighbours upon very slight occasions, and often upon meere suggestions.

It is a common practice amonge many of them, that if they heare a man hathe suspected his neïghoor, they will provoke him to sue him, and the Atturnye will undertake the suite and will be at all the charges, till it be ended, and if it goe with his client then he will please him selfe but if he misse, or that it be compounded (which the Atturnye will hardly yeild to) then comes a writt upon his poore clientes backe for charges. . . .

5

Correspondence, 1624-1629

Numerous letters to and from Winthrop give insight into the life he led in England. Only a few can be printed here. The first has been selected as typical of the letters to his wife Margaret at mid-decade, the remainder as indicative of his trend from engagement in the English scene to alienation.

Document 5-a†

John to Margaret Winthrop, November 26, 1624

My Sweet Wife, I blesse the Lorde for his continued blessinge upon thee and our familye: and I thanke thee for thy kinde Lettres: But I knowe not what to saye for my selfe: I should mende and growe a better husband havinge the helpe and example of so good a wife, but I growe still worse: I was wonte heeretofore, when I was longe absent, to make some supplye with volumes of Lettres but I can scarce afforde thee a few lines: well there is no helpe but by enlarginge thy patience, and strengthninge thy good opinion of him, who loves thee as his owne soule, and should count it his greatest Affliction to live without thee: but because thou art so deare to him, he must choose rather to leave thee for a tyme, than to enjoye thee: I am sorrye I must still prolonge thy expectation, for I cannot come forth of London till Tuesdaye at soonest; the Lorde blesse and keepe thee and all ours and sende us a joyfull meetinge. So I kisse my sweet wife and rest Thy faithfull husband
Jo: Winthrop

Document 5-b

John Winthrop to Sir Robert Crane, January 14, 1626

Right Worthy Sir, Since I parted from you, I heard of a motion made by a gent[leman] of our Countye for Electing Sir Robert Nanton the master of the wardes to be one of the knightes for our Countye, so as havinge Conference with my broth: Down: about it, we have thought fitt to move your selfe and some others in it, I suppose there wilbe no exception against him, except for that he is a privie Counseller, which may easyly be removed by consideration of what he hathe formerly suffered for the Common-wealthe: and you well knowe of what use the favour and helpe of suche an honorable person may be, in the Causes of our Countye especially for our

†Documents 5-a to 5-i—From: Massachusetts Historical Society, *Winthrop Papers* (Boston, 1929-47), vol. I, pp. 315-16, 324-25, 340, 379; vol. II, pp. 58-59, 66-69, 74-75, 78-79, 91-92. Reprinted by permission of the Society.

Clothiers; as for his greatnesse that need not discourage them, for besides, that I knowe, he beares a speciall affection to our Countrye, (and would take it as the greatest honor that could befall him in this kinde, to have this testimonye of their love to him againe) I dare undertake, for their readye accesse to him at tymes convenient;

If you approve of this motion, I desire you would please to propounde it to the other gent[lemen] at Sessions, and if you thinke good to write to Ipswich or any other place about it, the master shalbe certified of your care and paines about it, who (I knowe) will take it verye kindly from you, and will be thankfull to you; for a meet person to be joyned with him, I could wishe your selfe would take it upon you, but if you like to refuse, some eminent and discreet person would be thought of; if it were one of the deputy Leiut[enan]tes it were the better, and it might be of good use if some of the gent[lemen] of the leiute[nan]tie were moved for their assistance: If you please you may thinke of Sir Nath: Barnardiston tho he be out of the Countye.

Having diverse lettres to dispatche I cannot write to you as I desire, for news there is none certaine but of the putting of the coronation till maye and then to be performed privately: and of order taken with the Bishops to proceed with the Papists by Ecc[lesias]ti[c]all Censures: and so with remembrance of my humble service to you, I take leave and rest allwayes yours to be commanded

John Winthrop.

Document 5-c

John Winthrop Jr. to John Winthrop, January 15, 1627

Most Loving Father, my duty remembred to your selfe my mother and Grandmother with my love to my brothers and the rest of our freindes. The occation of my sending thus hastily is this. that wheras Mr. Lattimer one of the Atturnies of the Court of Wardes is yesterday dead so as now that place is void my uncle Downing willed me to give you speedy notice of it and desire you to come up with all speed you can to London for the master is now out of towne and doth not returne till Saterday nexte and he would have you be here before his comming home that you might ride some way out of towne to meete him because he feareth that if it be not granted presently at his comming home, or before, the Kinges or Dukes letter may be a meanes to make it be disposed of some other way. therefore if you have a mind to it my uncle thinkes it will be your best course to be heare upon friday at furthest and he will use all the meanes he can to obteyne it for you and in the meane tyme if he can by any meanes he will write into the country to the master about it. Thus hoping to see you soone at London I desire your prayers and blessing and so rest Your Obedient Sonne

John Winthrop

Document 5-d

Margaret to John Winthrop, ca. February 4, 1628

My Most Deare and Loveinge Husband I doe blesse and prayse god for the continuance of your health, and for the safe delivery of my good sister [Lucy] Downinge, it was very welcom Nuse to us. I thanke the lord wee are all heare resonably well my pore Stephen is up to day. Ame hath had a very sore Ague but is well againe. I hope the lorde will heare our prayers and be pleased to stay his hand in this visitasion which if he please to doe we shall have great cause of thankfulnesse. but I desire in this and all other things to submit unto his holy will, it is the lord let him doe what semeth good in his owne eyse. he will doe nothinge but that shall be for our good if we had harts to thust [*sic*, trust] in him. ... I am sorye for the hard condishtion of Rochell. the lord helpe them and fite for them and then none shall prevayle against them or overcome them. in vaine thay fite against the lorde who is a myty god and will destroye all his enimyes and now my deare husband I have nothinge but my dearest affections to send thee with many thankes for my [*sic*, your] kinde letters prayinge you to except a little for a greate deale my will is good but that I want abilite how to show and expresse it to thee as I desire I pray remember me to my brothers and sisters and tel my brother Foones I thanke him for the thinges he sent, and so I bid my good husband farwell and commite him to god Your loveinge and obedient wife

Margaret Winthrope

Document 5-e

John Winthrop to John Winthrop Jr., February 25, 1628

Sonne Jo: I prayse God we came home well on thursdaye at night and this daye I was at the choyce of our knightes [Members of Parliament] at Ipswich what our successe was you may knowe by my lettre to either of your unckles. as like wise for other affaires. ... I would be lothe to come up before the terme except there be necessitye. yet I thincke to be there about a weeke before, because my horse must be at Houndsloe heathe the 23 of Aprill, and likewise to take order about my removall, which I am now (in a manner) resolved off, if God shall dispose for us accordingly: for my charge heere grows verye heavye, and I am wearye of these journies to and fro, so as I will either remove or putt off my office. I would have you enquire about for a house at tower-hill or some suche open place, or if I cant be provided so neere, I will make tryall of Thistleworthe [Isleworth]: I would be neere churche and some good schoole. If you can finde how to sende to your brother Hen: let me knowe that I may provide shoes etc: for him, and for other thinges I will leave them to your care. We are all in good healthe (I prayse God) Deane hathe had the smale poxe, but laye not by it, and Sam[uel] was verye sicke, and in great danger, but God hathe delivered him. your grandmother and mother salute and blesse you: the lorde blesse guide and prosper you in all your wayes, that you may feare him, and cleave to him, and so consecrate your life and youthe to his service, as your life may be of use for his glorye and the good of others. farewell. your lovinge father

Jo: Winthrop

Document 5-f

John to Henry Winthrop, January 30, 1629

Sonne Henrye, It is my daylye care to commende you to the Lorde, that he would please to putt his true feare into your heart and the faythe of the Lorde Jesus Christ, that you may be saved, and that your wayes may be pleasinge in his sight: I wishe also your outward prosperitye, so farre as may be for your good. I have been sicke, these 7: or 8: weekes neere unto deathe, but the Lord hathe had mercye on me, to restore me, yet I am not able to goe abroad: I sent you [in Barbados] by Capt. Powell a Lettre and in it a note of suche thinges as I likewise sent you by him, in a Cheste with 2 lockes, whereof the keyes were delivered to his Brother who went master of the shippe: the thinges cost me about 35 *li.* but as yet I have received nothinge towardes it. I sent diverse tymes to Capt. Powell about your Tobacko, but my man could never see it, but had answeare I should have it, or mony for it: but there was 10: pounde of it by your appointment to be delivered to one, and the worthe of 4 *li.* to another, which made me, that I knew not what course to take: besides I founde, by the rolles you sent to me and to your unckles, that it was verye ill conditioned, fowle, full of stalkes and evill coloured, and your unckle Fones takinge the Judgment of divers Grocers, none of them would give five shillinges a pounde for it: I desired Capt. Powell (cominge one daye to see me) that he would helpe me with monye for it, which he promised to doe, but as yet I heare not from him. I would have sent you some other thinges by Mr. Randall, but in truethe I have no monye, and I am so farre in debt allreadye to bothe your unckles, as I am ashamed to borrowe any more. I have disbursed a great deale of monye for you more then my estate will beare: I payde for your debtes since you went above 30 *li.* besides 4: *li.* 10 *s.* to Annett and Dixon, and now 35 *li.* except you sende commoditye to rayse monye I can supplye you no further: I have many other children that are unprovided, and I see my life is uncertain. I mervaile at your great undertakinges, havinge no meanes, and knowinge how muche I am in debt allreadye. Salomon saythe he who hasteth to be rich shall surely come to poverty: it had been more wisdome, and better becomminge your youthe, to have conteined your selfe in a moderate course, for your 3: yeares, and by that tyme, by your owne gettinges and my helpe, you might have been able to have doone somewhat, but this hathe been allwayes the fruit of your vaine overreachinge minde, which wilbe your overthrowe, if you attaine not more discreation and moderation with your yeares: I doe wonder upon what grounde you should be ledd into so grosse an error, as to thinke, that I could provide 10: such men as you write for and disburse a matter of 200 *li.* (when I owe more allreadye, then I am able to paye, without sale of my lande) and to doe this at some 2: or 3: monthes warninge: well I will write no more of these thinges: I praye God make you more wise and sober, and bringe you home in peace in his due tyme. If I receive mony for your Tobacco before mr. Randall goe, I will sende you somethinge els, otherwise you must be content to staye till I can. If you sende over any more Tobacco, take order it may be delivered to me, and if you will have any to have shares out of it, let me have the disposinge of it, for this last course of yours makes me jealous of your intent, as I can be no lesse, when you gave me suche particular direction for the best improvement of it, and yet underhand appoint another to dispose of a good parte of it: well, enough of this: your brother (as I wrote to you) hath been in the Levant above this halfe yeare, and I looke not for him before a yeare more. your freindes heere are all in healthe: your unckles and Auntes commende them to you, but they will take none of your Tobacko: ... Sir Nath: Barnardiston and Sir W[illia]m Springe, are knightes of the Parliament for Suffolk, all the gent[lemen] have been longe since sett at libertye. Sir Francis Barington is at rest in the Lorde. Sir Hen: Mildmay of Graces is Sherife of Essex and mr. Gurdon for Suffolk: I have stayed sendinge my Lettre above a weeke since I wrote it, expectinge some mony from Capt. Powell according to his promise, that I might have sent you some other thinges, but I heere of none: therefore I will ende, and deferre till some other occasion: so againe I commend you to the blessinge protection and direction of the Lord and rest your lovinge father

Jo: Winthrop.

Document 5-g

Emmanuel Downing to John Winthrop, March 6, 1629

My Good Brother, I am glad you retorned home soe well, and founde them soe there;

the newes yeasterday upon thexchange was, that the Dutch have taken the second parte of the Spaynishe plate Fleete

One [*sic*, On] Monday morning the Parliament mett, and presently soe soone as they were sett there came a messenger mr. Maxwell of the bedchamber from the king to dissolve the howse, mr. Litleton tendred a Demonstrance to the Speaker to be read, he refused, the howse comaunded him, he weepes and offers to goe out of the chayre, he was by force kept in, manie cryed out with him to the barr and choose an other in his place, they comaunded the Serjeant to lock the dore, ere the Messenger entred, he durst not, up riseth a Burgesse [member] and offers his service, they all willed him lock the dore and bring away the key, they comaunded the Clarke to reade yt, he answeared that he was to reade nothing but what was past and entred in the booke, then mr. Litleton goes into the next roome and burnes the Demonstrance, up riseth Hollace one of the lord of Clares sonns, and declares to the howse the somme and heades of the Demonstrance, to this effect; that all those are enemyes to this Church and Common w[ealth] that seekes to bring in these new opynions, And that those merchantes shalbe reputed enemyes to this state that shall yeald tonnadge and poundadge before yt be graunted in Parli[ament]. And the Conclusion was most sharpe and cruell against the Lo[rd] Trea[surer] and the B[isho]p of Wynchester;

One Tuseday mr. Seldon, mr. Litleton, and 3 more were sent to the Tower, Sir Peter Heymond and 2 others to the gatehowse, 8 more sent for, all are close prisoners that are comitted, mr. Seldons study is sealed up, this morning I was told that there be 2 barges attending at Whytehall to carry some noblemen to the tower, and that the Customhowse dores are shutt up for that the officers dare not sett to demaund Custome, I heard yeasterday at Char[ing] Crosse that the Customers of Lynn were beaten out of the Customhowse, the good lord torne all to a good yssue, soe with myne and my wives dewty to my mother with our love to your selfe and my good sister etc. I rest your verie loving brother

Em: Downinge.

Document 5-h

Thomas Fones to John Winthrop, April 2, 1629

My Good Brother, I did not write last week being so lame I could not feed my self with any hand nor stir out of my chamber and am still very weak so that though I have much to write I have litle ability of Body or Mind being overwhelmed with trobles and aflictiones on all sydes and Increased exceedingly by those from whom I have deserved better but . . . yet thus far my desire to keep my Nephew your sonne [Henry] from much expence and rioutous company made me for your sake most and in him as a member of yow to give him entertaynment to lodge and diet in my howse when I had no small troble with him and such as he brought dayly so that yf he were within my howse was like an Inne and I lodged and dieted a man he entertayned a papist till iii dayes since perceav[ing] him to have accese to a priest in newgate I durst give him no longer Intertaynment but I will yow know the Issue and the requitall of my kindnes your sonne hath wooed and wonne my daughter Besse for a wyfe and they both pretend to have proceeded so far that there is no recalling of yt at least promise of Mariage and all without my knowledg or consent what grief this is to me I leave yt to your consideracion being no fitt mach for ether of them. I will not multiply argumentes agaynst my Nephew being your sonne but his hart I see is much to bigg for his estates: he hath now made him a skarlet suit and cloke which is lined through with plush which I believe he owes for besydes what more so that I doubt the five pownd yow wrote me to deliver him had [illegible] and therfor I have yet done nothing but paid xx s. my daughter borrowed for him when I could come by no mony my wyfe being not within: for his other affayres I know no certainty of any thing but I think he will write and for publick busines my mind is so Laden with my own and I so bad a writer I cannot Informe yow only I desier yow to receave my rent of Haxall and yf Gage retorne not mine to London of him likewise and let me heare your Judgment in the matter before written what wee shall do and now being very weary of wrighting and having not heard of yow this weeke I conclude with my harty love remembred to yow and yours not forgetting my good Mother and shall remayne your Loving brother

Tho: Fones.

[P.S.] I cannot write yow the many trobles of my mind what to do for my Nephew sayes playnly yf he cannot have my good will to have my daughter he will have her without: and though I have entreated him to forbeare my howse a while he will not but comes and stayes at unfitting howres he lay here till last night: I am sure he is in debt for his owne occasions, I doubt far and I feare engaged for others whose company he useth and they have had thinges so common betweene them of whom formerly I have given him frendly warning but I am weak and cannot I see now be master in myne owne howse and tis hard medling betweene the barke and the tree for yf he were not so neare allied to me and the sonne of him whom I so respect I could hardly beare such braving oppositions in mine owne howse: but I long to heare from yow for I doubt he will draw hir forth of mine owne howse and soddaynly marry hir without any Scrupules

Document 5-i

John to Margaret Winthrop, May 15, 1629

My Good Wife, I prayse the Lorde for the wished newes of thy wellfare and of the rest of our Companye, and for the continuance of ours heer: it is a great favour, that we may enjoye so much comfort and peace in these so evill and declining tymes and when the increasinge of our sinnes gives us so great cause to looke for some heavye Scquorge and Judgment to be comminge upon us: the Lorde hath admonished, threatened, corrected, and astonished us, yet we growe worse and worse, so as his spirit will not allwayes strive with us, he must needs give waye to his furye at last: he hath smitten all the other Churches before our eyes, and hath made them to drinke of the bitter cuppe of tribulation, even unto death; we sawe this, and humbled not ourselves, to turne from our evill wayes, but have provoked him more then all the nations rounde about us: therefore he is turninge the cuppe towards us also, and because we are the last, our portion must be, to drinke the verye dreggs which remaine: my deare wife, I am veryly perswaded, God will bringe some heavye Affliction upon this lande, and that speedylye: but be of good Comfort, the hardest that can come shall be a meanes to mortifie this bodye of Corruption, which is a thousand tymes more dangerous to us then any outward tribulation, and to bringe us into neerer communion with our Lo: Jes: Christ, and more Assurance of his kingdome. If the Lord seeth it wilbe good for us, he will provide a shelter and a hidinge place for us and ours as a Zoar for Lott, Sarephtah for his prophet etc: if not, yet he will not forsake us: though he correct us with the roddes of men, yet if he take not his mercye and lovinge kindnesse from us we shalbe safe. He onely is allsufficient, if we have him, we have all thinges: if he seeth it not good, to cutt out our portion in these thinges belowe equall to the largnesse of our desires, yet if he please to frame our mindes to the portion he allottes us, it wilbe as well for us.

I thanke thee for thy kinde lettre, I am goinge to Westm[inster], and must heere breake of. I would have my sonne H[enry] to be heere on teusdaye that I may goe out of towne on wensdaye or thursdaye next. If marye her gowne be made I will send it downe by Smith this weeke, or els next, with other thinges: all our freindes heer are indifferent well, and desire to be comended to thee, so with my hearty salut[ation]s to all our freindes with thee, my love and blessinge to my sonnes and daughteres, In very much hast, I ende and commende thee and all ours to the gratious protection and blessinge of the Lorde so I kisse my sweet wife, and thinke longe till I see thee farewell. Thine

Jo: Winthrop.

6

On "The Lawfulness of Removing out of England"

The American alternative which would attract Winthrop from old England to new was offered in conversations and pamphlets. What follows is a letter printed as part of a 1622 pamphlet describing the settlement of Plymouth by the Pilgrims. Signed simply "R.C.," the author is presumed to be Robert Cushman, who had sailed to New England on the *Mayflower* in 1620 and returned in 1621 to act as the Pilgrims' "business agent." Cushman titled the letter: "Reasons and Considerations Touching the Lawfulness of Removing out of England into the Parts of America."

Document †

Forasmuch as many Exceptions are daily made against the going into, and inhabiting of, foreign desert places; to the hinderances of Plantations abroad and the increase of distractions at home: it is not amiss that some (which have been Ear witnesses of the Exceptions made; and are Agents, or Abettors, of such Removals and Plantations) do seek to give content to the World, in all things that they possibly can.

And although most of the opposites are such as either dream of raising their fortunes here, to that than which there is nothing more unlike[ly]; or such as affecting their homeborn country so vehemently as that they had rather, with all their friends, beg, yea starve in it, than undergo a little difficulty in seeking abroad: yet are there some who (out of doubt, in tenderness of conscience and fear to offend GOD, by running before they be called) are straitened; and do straiten others from going into foreign Plantations.

For whose cause, especially; I have been drawn, out of my good affection to them, to publish some Reasons that might give them content and satisfaction; and also stay and stop the willful and witty caviller. . . .

And so here falleth in our question, How a man that is here born and bred, and hath lived some years, may remove himself into another country?

†From. *A Relation, or Journal of the Beginning and Proceedings of the English Plantation settled at Plymouth, in New England* (London, 1622), in *The Story of the Pilgrim Fathers, 1606-1623* ed., Edward Arber (Boston and New York, 1897), pp. 495-505.

Answer. I answer, A man must not respect only to live and do good to himself; but he should see where he can live to do most good to others: for, as one saith, "He whose living is but for himself; it is time he were dead."

Some men there are who, of necessity, must here live; as being tied to duties, either to Church, Common Wealth, household, kindred, &c. But others, and that many, who do no good in none of those [callings], nor can do none; as being not able, or not in favour, or as wanting opportunity: and living as outcasts, nobodies, eyesores; eating but for themselves; teaching but themselves; and doing good to none, either in soul or body; and so pass over days, years, and months; yea, so live and so die.

Now such should lift up their eyes and see, Whether there be not some other place and country to which they may go, to do good: and have use towards others, of that knowledge, wisdom, humanity, reason, strength, skill, faculty, &c.; which GOD hath given them for the service of others, and his own glory?

But not to pass the bounds of modesty so far as to name any, though I confess I know many who sit here still, with their talent in a napkin, having notable endowments, both of body and mind; and might do great good if they were in some places; which here do none, nor can do none: and yet, through fleshly fear, niceness, straitness of heart, &c., sit still and look on; and will not hazard a dram of health, nor a day of pleasure, nor an hour of rest, to further the knowledge and salvation of the sons of ADAM in that New World; where a drop of the knowledge of CHRIST is most precious, which is here not set by. Now what shall we say to such a Profession of CHRIST, to which is joined no more denial of a man's self?

Objection. But some will say, What right have I to go live in the heathen's country?

Answer. Letting pass the ancient discoveries, contracts, and agreements which our Englishmen have, long since, made in those parts; together with the acknowledgement of the Histories and Chronicles of other nations; who profess the land of America, from Cape de Florida unto the Bay of Canada ... is proper to the King of England. Yet letting that pass, lest I be thought to meddle further than it concerns me, or further than I have discerning: I will mention such things as are within my reach, knowledge, sight, and practice, since I have travailed in these affairs.

And first, Seeing we daily pray for the conversion of the heathens; we must consider, Whether there be not some ordinary means and course for us to take to convert them: or whether prayer for them, be only referred to GOD's extraordinary work from heaven? Now it seemeth unto me, that we ought also to endeavour and use the means to convert them: and the means cannot be used, unless we go to them, or they come to us. To us, they cannot come: our land is full. To them, we may go: their land is empty.

This then is a sufficient reason to prove our going thither to live, lawful. Their land is spacious and void, and there are few: and [they] do but run over the grass, as do also the foxes and wild beasts. They are not industrious: neither have art, science, skill, or faculty to use either the land, or the commodities of it; but all spoils, rots, and is marred, for want of manuring, gathering, ordering, &c. As the ancient Patriarchs therefore removed from straiter places into more roomthy, where the land lay idle and waste, and none used; though there dwelt inhabitants by them, as Gen. xiii. 6, 11, 12 and xxxiv. 21, and xli. 20: so is it lawful now to take a land, which none useth; and make use of it. . . . And as it is a common land or unused, and undressed country; so we have it, by common consent, composition, and agreement [of various Indian leaders]. . . .

It being then, first, a vast and empty chaos; secondly, acknowledged the right of our Sovereign King; thirdly, by a peaceable composition . . . I see not who can doubt and call in question the lawfulness of inhabiting or dwelling there; but that it may be as lawful for such, as are not tied upon some special occasion here, to live there as well as here. Yea, and as the enterprise is weighty and difficult: so the honour is more worthy, to plant a rude wilderness, to enlarge the honour and fame of our dread Sovereign; but chiefly to display the efficacy and power of the Gospel, both in zealous preaching, Professing, and wise walking under it, before the faces of these poor blind infidels.

As for such as object the tediousness of the voyage thither; the danger of pirates' robbery, of the savages' treachery, &c.; these are but lions in the way: and it were well for such men, if they were in heaven. For who can shew them a place in this world, where iniquity shall not compass them at the heels? or where they shall have a day without grief? or a lease of life, for a moment? And who can tell but GOD, what dangers may lie at our doors, even in our native country? or what plots may be abroad? or when GOD will cause our sun to go down at noonday? and, in the midst of our peace and security, lay upon us some lasting scourge for our so long neglect and contempt of his most glorious Gospel?

Objection. But we have here great peace, plenty of the Gospel, and many sweet delights and variety of comforts.

Answer. True indeed, and far be it from us to deny and diminish the least of these mercies. But have we rendered unto GOD thankful obedience for this long peace, whilst other peoples have been at war? Have we not rather murmured, repined, and fallen at jars amongst ourselves; whilst our peace hath lasted with foreign Power? Were there ever more suits in law, more envy, contempt, and reproach, than now a days? ABRAHAM and LOT departed asunder, when there fell a breach betwixt them; which was occasioned by the straitness of the land: and, surely, I am persuaded that howsoever the frailities of men are principal in all contentions, yet the straitness of the place is such, as each man is fain to pluck his means, as it were, out of his neighbour's throat. There is such pressing and oppressing, in town and country, about farms, trades, traffic, &c.; so as a man can hardly anywhere set up a trade, but he shall pull down two of his neighbours.

The towns abound with young tradesmen and the hospitals are full of the ancient. The country is replenished with new farmers; and the almhouses are filled with old labourers. Many there are who get their living with bearing burdens; but more are fain to burden the land with their whole bodies. Multitudes get their means of life by prating; and so do numbers more, by begging. Neither come these straits upon men always through intemperancy, ill husbandry, indiscretion, &c., as some think: but even the most wise sober and discreet men go often to the wall; when they have done their best. Wherein, as GOD's Providence swayeth all, so it is easy to see, That the straitness of the place, having in it so many strait hearts, cannot but produce such effects more and more. So as every indifferent minded man should be ready to say, with father ABRAHAM, "Take thou, the right hand; and I will take the left!" Let us not thus oppress, straiten, and afflict one another! but seeing there is a spacious land, the way to which is through the sea, we will end this difference in a day!

That I speak nothing about the bitter contention that hath been about Religion, by writing disputing and inveighing earnestly one against another: the heat of which zeal, if it were turned against the rude barbarism of the heathens, it might do more good in a day than it hath done here in many years. Neither of the little love to the Gospel, and profit which is made by the Preachers in most places; which might easily drive the zealous to the heathens: who, no doubt, if they had but a drop of that knowledge, which here flyeth about the streets, would be filled with exceeding great joy and gladness, as that thay would even pluck the Kingdom of Heaven by violence; and take it, as it were, by force. . . .

The greatest let [hindrance] that is yet behind is, The sweet fellowship of friends, and the satiety of bodily delights.

But can there be two nearer friends almost, than ABRAHAM and LOT; or than PAUL and BARNABAS? And yet, upon as little occasions as we have here, they departed asunder; two of them being Patriarchs of the Church of old, the others, the Apostles of the Church which is new. . . .

Neither must men take so much thought for the flesh as not to be pleased, except they can pamper their bodies with variety of dainties. Nature is content with little: and health is much endangered by mixtures upon the stomach. The delights of the palate do often inflame the vital parts; as the tongue setteth afire the whole body.

Secondly. Varieties here are not common to all; but many good men are glad to snap at a crust. The rent-taker lives on sweet morsels; but the rent-payer eats a dry crust often with watery eyes: and it is nothing to say, what some one of a hundred hath; but what the bulk, body, and comminalty hath—which, I warrant you, is short enough.

And they also which now live so sweetly; hardly will their children attain to that priviledge, but some circumventor or other will oustrip them, and make them sit in the dust: to which men are brought in one Age [lifetime]; but cannot get out of it again, in seven generations.

To conclude. Without all partiality, the present consumption which groweth upon us here (whilst the land groaneth under so many close-fisted and unmerciful men), being compared with the easiness, plainness, and plentifulness in living, in those remote parts; may quickly persuade any man to a liking of this course, and to practice a removal. Which being done by honest, godly and industrious men; they shall be there right heartily welcome: but for others of dissolute and profane life, their rooms are better than their companies. For if here, where the Gospel hath been so long and plentifully taught, they are yet frequent in such vices as the heathen would shame to speak of: what will they be, when there is less restraint in word and deed?

My only suit to all men is, That, whether they live here or there, they would learn to use this world as [if] they used it not; keeping faith and a good conscience both with GOD and men: that when the Day of Account shall come, they may come forth as good and fruitful servants; and freely be received, and enter into the joy of their Master.

7

"Generall Considerations for the Plantation"

Winthrop's public rationalization of his decision began at a meeting at Bury St. Edmunds on August 12, 1629. His notes for the meeting (presumably elaborated upon afterwards) have come down to us in several versions for copies were apparently circulated. The notes are in two parts, a series of "Generall considerations for the plantation in New England" and (Document 8) "Perticular Considerations in the Case of J:W:".

Document†

1. It wilbe a service to the Churche of great Consequence to carrye the Gospell into those partes of the world, and to rayse a bullwarke against the kingdom of Antichrist which the Jesuites labour to reare up in all places of the worlde.

2. All other Churches of Europe are brought to desolation, and it cannot be, but the like Judgment is comminge upon us: and who knows, but that God hathe provided this place, to be a refuge for manye, whom he meanes to save out of the general destruction?

3. This lande growes wearye of her Inhabitantes, so as man which is the most pretious of all Creatures, is heere more vile and base, then the earthe they treade upon: so as children neighbours and freindes (especi[ally] if they be poore) are rated the greatest burdens, which if things were right, would be the cheifest earthly bless[ings].

4. We are growne to that height of Intemperance in all excesse of Ryot, as no mans estate all most will suffice to keepe sayle with his equalls: and he that fayles in it, must live in scorn and contempt: hence it comes, that all artes and trades are carried in that deceiptfull and unrighteous course, as it is allmost imposs[ible] for a good and upright man to maintaine his charge and live comfortably in any of them.

5. The fountains of learninge and Relig[ion] are so corrupted, as (besides the unsupport[able] chardge of their educat[ion]) most Children, even the best wittes and of fayrest hopes, are perverted corrupted and utterly overthrowne by the multitude of evill examples and the licentious government of those seminaryes.

†From: Massachusetts Historical Society, *Winthrop Papers* (Boston, 1929-47), vol. II, pp. 114-17. Reprinted by permission of the Society.

6. The whole earthe is the Lordes garden: and he hathe given it to the sons of men to be tilld and improved by them: why then should we stand striving heere for places of habitation etc. (many men spending as muche labor and cost to recover or keepe sometyme an Acre or 2 of lande, as would procure him many C [hundred] acres as good or better in another place) and in the mene tyme suffer whole countrys as fruitfull and convenient for the use of man, to lye waste without any improvement?

7. What can be a better worke and more honorable and worthy a Christian then to helpe rayse and supporte a partic[ular] Churche while it is in the infancye, and to joine our forces with suche a Companye of faithfull people, as by a tymely assistance maye growe stronge and prosper, and for want of it may be putt to great hazard, if not wholly ruined?

8. If suche as are knowne to be godly and live in wealthe and prosperitye heere, shall forsake all this to joine themselves to this Churche, and to runne the hazard with them of a harde and meane condition, it wilbe an example of great use, bothe for removinge the schandale of worldly and sinister respectes to give more life to the Faithe of Godes people in their prayers for the plantation, and allso to incourage others to joyne the more willingly in it.

Ob[jection I: It wilbe a great wronge to our owne Churche and Countrye, to take awaye the good people, and we shall laye it the more open to the Judgment feared.

Ans[wer] I: the number wilbe nothing in respecte of those that are lefte: 2 many that live to no use heere, more then for their owne private familys, may be imployed to a more com[mon] good in another place: 3: suche as are of noe use heere, may yet be so imployed, as the Church shall receive no losse: and since Christes tyme the Chur[ch] is to be considered as universall, without distinction of countrys, so as he that dothe good in any one place serves the Church in all places in regarde of the unitye. lastly it is the revealed will of God, that the Gospell should be preached to all nations: and thoughe we knowe not, whither the Indians will receive it or not, yet it is a good worke, to observe Godes will in offering it to them, for God shall have Glory by it, though they refuse it.

Ob. 2. We have feared a Judgment a longe tyme, but yet we are safe, soe it were better to staye till it come, and either we may flye then, or if we be overtaken in it we may well contente our selves to suffer with suche a Churche as ours is.

Ans. It is like that this consideration made the Churches beyonde the seas (as the Pal[atinate] Rochell etc.) to sitt still at home, and not look out for shelter while they might have founde it: but the woefull spectacle of their ruine, may teache us more wisdome, to avoyde the plague when it is foreseene, and not to tarrye, as they did, till it overtake us: if they were now at their former libertye, we may be sure, they would take other Course for their safety: and though most of them had misca[rried] in their escape, yet it had not been halfe so miserable to them selves, nor scandalous to Religion, as this desperate backslidinge, and abjuringe the truethe, which many of the auncient professors amonge them, and the whole posteryty that remaine are now plunged into.

Ob. 3. We have heere a fruitfull lande with peace and plenty of all thinges etc.

Ans. our superfluities excepted we are like to be followed with as good con[sequences] remaininge there in a shorte tyme, and be far from many temptations meet with here. yet we must leave all this abondance, if it be not taken from us: and when we are in our graves it wilbe all one to have lived in plentye or penurye, whither we had dyed in a bedd of downe, or a lock of strawe, and onely this is the advantage of a meane condition, that it is at more freedom to dye and the lesse comfort any hathe in the things of this world, the more liberty and desire he may have to laye up treasure in heaven.

Ob. 4. But we may perishe by the waye or when we come there, either hanginge hunger or the sworde etc., and how uncomfortable it would be to see our wives children and freindes come to suche misery by our occasion?

Ans. Suche ob[jection] savours to muche of the flesh: who can save him selfe or his familye from calamitys heere? if this course be warrantable we must trust Godes providence for these thinges, either he will keepe these evills from us, or will dispose them for our good, and enable us to beare them.

Ob. 5. But what warrant have we to take that lande which is and hathe been of longe tyme possessed by other sonnes of Adam?

sol. That which is com[mon] to all is proper to none, these salvadge peoples ramble over muche lande without title or propertye: 2: there is more then enough for them and us; 3: God hathe consumed the natives with a miraculous plague, wherby a great parte of the Country is left voyde of Inh[abita]ntes. 4. We shall come in with good leave of the natives.

Ob. 6. we should yet send yonge ones, and suche as may best be spared, and not of our best min[isters] and magistrates.

sol. It is a greater worke and requires more skillfull artizans, to laye the foundation of a newe building, then to uphould or repaire one that is ready built: if great things be attempted by weake instrum[en]tes, the effects willbe answerable:

Ob. 7. We see those plantations, which have been formerly made, succeeded ill.

Ans. the fruit of any publ[ic] designe is not to be discerned by the im[me]diate successe, it may appeare in tyme, that they were all to good use. 2: there were great and fundamentall errors in the other which are like to be avoyded in this: for I: their maine ende [and] purpose was carnall and not religious; they aymed cheifly at profitt, and not the propagating of Religion. 2: they used unfitt instrumentes, a multitude of Rude and misgoverned persons the verye scomme of the lande. 3: they did not establish a right forme of Gover[n]ment.

8

"Perticular Considerations in the Case of J:W:"

Document†

1. It is come to that issue, as, in all probabilitye, the wellfare of the plantation depends upon my assistance: for the maine pillers of it beinge gentlemen of highe qualitye, and eminent partes, bothe for wisdome and godlinesse, are determined to sitt still, if I deserte them.

2. my meanes heere are so shortned (now my 3 eldest sonnes are come to age) as I shall not be able to continue in this place and imployment where I now am: and a souldier may with honor quitt his ground rather then be forced from it and with what comfort can I live with 7: or 8: servants in that place and condition where for many years I have spent 3: or 400 *li* per an[num], and maintain as great a chardge? and if I should let passe this opportunitye, that talent which God hath bestowed on me for publike service, were like to be buried. [Inserted in the margin:] When a man is to wade throughe a deepe water, there is required tallnesse, as well as Courage, and if he findes it past his depth, and God open a gapp another waye, he may take it.

3. I have a lawfull callinge, outwarde, from the Cheife of the plantation, approved by godly and juditious divines: and inwarde by the inclination of mine owne heart to the worke: and there is in this the like mediate Call from the kings, which was in the other.

4. my wife and suche of my Children, as are come to yeares of discreation, are voluntaryly disposed to the same course.

5. In my youth I did seariously consecrate my life to the service of the Churche (intendinge the ministry) but was diverted from that course by the counsell of some, whose Judgment I did much reverence: but it hathe ofte troubled me since, so as I thinke I am the rather bounde to take the opportunitye for spendinge the small remainder of my tyme, to the best service of the Churche which I may.

It[em]. which way the streame of Gods providence leades a man to the greatest good, he may, nay he must goe.

†From: Massachusetts Historical Society, *Winthrop Papers* (Boston, 1929-47), vol. II, pp. 125-26. Reprinted by permission of the Society.

9

Winthrop's Answer to a Critic

There were many critics of Winthrop's decision. In answer to one (although we have only half the letter) Winthrop elaborated upon his reasons for going. It is perhaps as argumentative a letter as Winthrop ever wrote.

Document†

... which now lyes waste there, more plenty wilbe lefte to suche as remaine behinde.

3: For the 3: if it be a personall instance, it may best receive answere from such as it concerns, but as it may be extended to the estate of our Churche and Com[mon] w[ealth] let the grones and fears of Godes people give a silent answer: If our condition be good, why doe his Embassadours, turne their messages into complaintes and threatninges? why doe they so constantly denounce wrathe and judgment against us? why doe they pray so muche for healinge if we be not sicke? why doe their soules wepe in secret? and will not be comforted, if there be yet hope that our hurt may be healed? One Calfe set up in Israel removed the tabernacle out of the host, and for 2 God forsooke them for ever. . . . if it be thus with us, where then is the happinesse we should rest in? if we imytate Sodom in her pride and intemperance, if Laodicea in her lukewarmnesse, if Eph[esus] Sardis etc. in the sins for which their Candlesticke was removed, if the turks and other heathen in their abominations, yea if the Sinagogue of Antichrist in her superstition, where is yet the good should content us? but it may be it is to be found in the civill state; what means then the bleating of so many oppressed with wronge, that drink wormwood, for righteousnesse? why doe so many seely sheep that seeke shelter at the judgment seates returne without their fleeces? why meet we so many wandering ghostes in shape of men, so many spectacles of misery in all our streetes, our houses full of victuals, and our entryes of hunger-starved Christians? our shoppes full of riche wares, and under our stalles lye our own fleshe in nakednesse. . . .

For the Abiennes [Albigenses?] etc.: yet you will grant that it had been better suche had fled, for they may yet belonge to God, at least some of them, dothe not the history of the Churche give us many examples of the like, who have been renewed by repentance? and for the posteryty bothe of good and badde, they were in the Covenant, and a holy seed, and so suche as

†From: Massachusetts Historical Society, *Winthrop Papers* (Boston, 1929-47), vol. II, pp. 121-24. Reprinted by permission of the Society.

the Churche might have had good hope of, if they might have been brought up under the menes[?], yet we ascribe no suche vertue to the soile, therefore that Conclusion might have been spared.

For the Corruption in trade, I see it is not denyed, if it were, I would desire him to instance one (being fitt imployment for an ingenuous minde) wherein a man may looke for recompence sutable to his expence of tyme and industrye, except falshood be admitted to equall the ballance: And for that course of husbandry which Jacob and the patriarchs used, it was honourable and usefull in those tymes and Countryes, but not in ours, they had their lande for nothinge, if we should imploye our children in that waye now, their worke would soon eate up their stocks, and for your supposition of what redresse might be had in these thinges by the magistrate, [it] dothe not conclude that it shalbe, nor tye us to expect what you give us no grounde to hope for. we confesse indeed that the multitude of people is the glorye of a kinge, and to maintain these and imploye them to the more profit doth not diminish but increase his glorye. those which goe over remaine still his subjectes, they may multiply as fast there as heere, by their labour, more food and other provisions for life shalbe raysed abroad, and yet no whitt the lesse at home: so that it is likly the nayls shalbe somewhat shortened, and yet the flesh remaine wholl. . . .

I will insist upon this one Argument. A lande overburdened with people, may ease it self, by sending a parte into some other Countryes which lye wast and not replenished: but suche is the condition of our lande ergo: etc: the proposition I prove thus, God at first did not replenish the earthe with men, but gave them a general Commiss[ion] Gen: I: 28. encrease and multiply and replenish the earth and subdue it: the endes are naturall and double, that man may enjoye the fruit of the earth, and God may have his due glory from the Creature, which is imperfect while it lyes waste. the Assertion I thus prove (though I never heard it denyed) many of our people perish for want of sustenance and imployment, many others live miserably and not to the honor of so bountifull a housekeeper as the lord of heaven and earth is, through the scarcity of the fruites of the earth. the whole lande of the kingdom as it is reconed is scarce sufficient to give imployment to one half of the people: all our townes complain of the burden of poore people and strive by all menes to ridde any such as they have, and to keepe of such as would come to them, masters are forced by authority to entertaine servantes parentes to maintain their children, more strife there is and expence between parishes to get ridde of some of their poore, then would suffice to maintaine them many yeares, and to fill up this cloud of testimonyes. . . . I must tell you, that our deare mother findes her famyly so overcharged, as she hathe been forced to denye harbour to her owne children, witnesse the statute against Cottages and inmates, so that whither it be of necessity or by inevitable accident, this is our condition, and no remedy appeares, so the assumption is proved and the argument standes good. as for those allusions resemblinge Davides longinge for a draught of water to this action, the thinges are so unlike, as neede no answere, your similitudes must have more legges if you will have them stande upright or prove any thinge.

Amonge all other difficultyes, the provision for your poore will prove a laberinth, because to preserve life in the weaker you must draw blood from the stronger yet you shall finde often thus, that gentle speeches, and a small releife from your owne hande, will prevaile muche with bothe partyes: and if thinges growe to an extremity as I feare they will soone, it will prove a savinge bargain. if popular tumultes should arise, which God forbide, remember the issue of the commotion of the pesantes in Germany. those base people were soone punished or subdued, but then were the riche men of the Countrye called to a reconinge, which cost many of them their lives and estates, wherof some did but looke on, and durst not releive them, and others relieved them against their willes, givinge a parte to save the rest: and so founde the proverbe true facile invenies etc: but these thinges are to highe for my concept, though not unfitt for your consideration. I have been over teadious, and bolde upon your gentlenesse, but my hearte is still full either of matter or affection, and I could vent it freely.

10

"A Modell of Christian Charity"

Aboard ship on the way to New England, Winthrop wrote one of the most famous of his works, a lay-sermon prepared for delivery to his fellow passengers. The hectic days of decision making and preparation for the voyage were behind him; the equally hectic days of New England settlement were yet to begin. Can we presume that in presenting this "modell" for the society to be built, with its stress on social "love" and unity, Winthrop was reflecting the underlying grievance—the felt absence of love and unity—which had brought about his alienation from the society he was leaving?

Document†

Christian Charity
A Modell Hereof.

God Almightie in his most holy and wise providence hath soe disposed of the Condicion of mankinde, as in all times some must be rich some poore, some highe and eminent in power and dignitie; others meane and in subjeccion.

THE REASON HEREOF.

I. REAS: *First,* to hold conformity with the rest of his workes, being delighted to shewe forthe the glory of his wisdome in the variety and differance of the Creatures and the glory of his power, in ordering all these differences for the preservacion and good of the whole, and the glory of his greatnes that as it is the glory of princes to have many officers, soe this great King will have many Stewards counting himselfe more honoured in dispenceing his guifts to man by man, then if hee did it by his owne immediate hand.

2. REAS: *Secondly,* That he might have the more occasion to manifest the worke of his Spirit: first, upon the wicked in moderateing and restraineing them: soe that the riche and mighty should not eate upp the poore, nor the poore, and dispised rise upp against theire superiors, and shake off theire yoake; 21y in the regenerate in exerciseing his graces in them,

†From: Massachusetts Historical Society, *Winthrop Papers* (Boston, 1929-47), vol. II, pp. 282-95. Reprinted by permission of the Society.

as in the greate ones, theire love mercy, gentlenes, temperance etc., in the poore and inferiour sorte, theire faithe patience, obedience etc:

3. REAS: *Thirdly*, That every man might have need of other, and from hence they might be all knitt more nearly together in the Bond of brotherly affeccion: from hence it appeares plainely that noe man is made more honourable then another or more wealthy etc., out of any perticuler and singuler respect to himselfe but for the glory of his Creator and the Common good of the Creature, Man; Therefore God still reserves the propperty of these guifts to himselfe as Ezek: 16. 17. he there calls wealthe his gold and his silver etc. Prov: 3.9. he claimes theire service as his due honour the Lord with thy riches etc. All men being thus (by divine providence) rancked into two sortes, riche and poore; under the first, are comprehended all such as are able to live comfortably by theire owne meanes duely improved; and all others are poore according to the former distribution. There are two rules whereby wee are to walke one towards another: JUSTICE and MERCY. These are allwayes distinguished in theire Act and in theire object, yet may they both concurre in the same Subject in eache respect; as sometimes there may be an occasion of shewing mercy to a rich man, in some sudden danger of distresse, and allsoe doeing of meere Justice to a poor man in regard of some perticuler contract etc. There is likewise a double Lawe by which wee are regulated in our conversacion one towardes another: in both the former respects, the lawe of nature and the lawe of grace, or the morrall lawe or the lawe of the gospell, to omitt the rule of Justice as not propperly belonging to this purpose otherwise then it may fall into consideracion in some perticuler Cases: By the first of these lawes man as he was enabled soe withall [is] commaunded to love his neighbour as himselfe upon this ground stands all the precepts of the morrall lawe, which concernes our dealings with men. To apply this to the works of mercy this lawe requires two things first that every man afford his help to another in every want or distresse Secondly, That hee performe this out of the same affeccion, which makes him carefull of his owne good according to that of our Saviour Math: [7.12] Whatsoever ye would that men should doe to you. This was practised by Abraham and Lott in entertaineing the Angells and the old man of Gibea. . . .

Having allready sett forth the practise of mercy according to the rule of gods lawe, it will be usefull to lay open the groundes of it allsoe being the other parte of the Commaundement and that is the affeccion from which this exercise of mercy must arise, the Apostle tells us that this love is the fullfilling of the lawe, not that it is enough to love our brother and soe noe further but in regard of the excellency of his partes gieving any motion to the other as the Soule to the body and the power it hath to sett all the faculties on worke in the outward exercise of this duty as when wee bid one make the clocke strike he doth not lay hand on the hammer which is the immediate instrument of the sound but setts on worke the first mover or maine wheele, knoweing that will certainely produce the sound which hee intends; soe the way to drawe men to the workes of mercy is not by force of Argument from the goodnes or necessity of the worke, for though this course may enforce a rationall minde to some present Act of mercy as is frequent in experience, yet it cannot worke such a habit in a Soule as shall make it prompt upon all occasions to produce the same effect but by frameing these affeccions of love in the hearte which will as natively bring forthe the other, as any cause doth produce the effect.

The diffinition which the Scripture gives us of love is this Love is the bond of perfection. First, it is a bond, or ligament. 21y, it makes the worke perfect. There is noe body but consistes of partes and that which knitts these partes together gives the body its perfeccion, because it makes eache parte soe contiguous to other as thereby they doe mutually participate with eache other, both in strengthe and infirmity in pleasure and paine, to instance in the most perfect of all bodies, Christ and his church make one body: the severall partes of this body considered aparte before they were united were as disproportionate and as much disordering as soe many contrary quallities or elements but when christ comes and by his spirit and love knitts all these partes to himselfe and each to other, it is become the most perfect and best proportioned body in the world Eph: 4. 16. "Christ by whome all the body being knitt together by every joynt for the furniture thereof according to the effectuall power which is in the measure of every perfeccion of partes a glorious body without spott or wrinckle the ligaments hereof being Christ or his love for Christ is love I John: 4. 8. Soe this definition is right Love is the bond of perfeccion.

From hence wee may frame these Conclusions.

I first all true Christians are of one body in Christ I. Cor. 12. 12. 13. 17. [27.] Ye are the body of Christ and members of [your?] parte.

21y. The ligamentes of this body which knitt together are love.

31y. Noe body can be perfect which wants its propper ligamentes.

41y. All the partes of this body being thus united are made soe contiguous in a speciall relacion as they must needes partake of each others strength and infirmity, joy, and sorrowe, weale and woe. I Cor: 12. 26. If one member suffers all suffer with it, if one be in honour, all rejoyce with it.

51y. This sensiblenes and Sympathy of each others Condicions will necessarily infuse into each parte a native desire and endeavour, to strengthen defend preserve and comfort the other.

To insist a little on this Conclusion being the product of all the former the truthe hereof will appeare both by precept and patterne i. John. 3. 10. yee ought to lay downe your lives for the brethren Gal: 6. 2. beare ye one anothers burthens and soe fulfill the lawe of Christ.

For patterns wee have that first of our Saviour whoe out of his good will in obedience to his father, becomeing a parte of this body, and being knitt with it in the bond of love, found such a native sensiblenes of our infirmities and sorrowes as hee willingly yeilded himselfe to deathe to ease the infirmities of the rest of his body and soe heale theire sorrowes: from the like Sympathy of partes did the Apostles and many thousands of the Saintes lay downe theire lives for Christ againe, the like wee may see in the members of this body among themselves. I. Rom. 9. Paule could have beene contented to have beene seperated from Christ that the Jewes might not be cutt off from the body: It is very observable which hee professeth of his affectionate part[ak]eing with every member: whoe is weake (saith hee) and I am not weake? whoe is offended and I burne not; and againe. 2 Cor: 7. 13. therefore wee are comforted because yee were comforted. of Epaphroditus he speaketh Phil: 2. 30. that he regarded not his owne life to [do] him service soe Phebe. and others are called the servantes of the Churche, now it is apparant that they served not for wages or by Constrainte but out of love, the like wee shall finde in the histories of the churche in all ages the sweete Sympathie of affeccions which was in the members of this body one towardes another, theire chearfullnes in serveing and suffering together how liberall they were without repineing harbourers without grudgeing and helpfull without reproacheing and all from hence they had fervent love amongst them which onely make[s] the practise of mercy constant and easie.

The next consideracion is how this love comes to be wrought: Adam in his first estate was a perfect modell of mankinde in all theire generacions, and in him this love was perfected in regard of the habit, but Adam Rent in himselfe from his Creator, rent all his posterity allsoe one from another, whence it comes that every man is borne with this principle in him, to love and seeke himselfe onely and thus a man continueth till Christ comes and takes possession of the soule, and infuseth another principle love to God and our brother. And this latter haveing continuall supply from Christ, as the head and roote by which hee is united get the predominency in the soule, soe by little and little expells the former I John 4. 7. love cometh of god and every one that loveth is borne of god, soe that this love is the fruite of the new birthe, and none can have it but the new Creature, now when this quallity is thus formed in the soules of men it workes like the Spirit upon the drie bones Ezek. 37. [7] bone came to bone, it gathers together the scattered bones of perfect old man Adam and knitts them into one body againe in Christ whereby a man is become againe a liveing soule.

The third Consideracion is concerning the exercise of this love, which is twofold, inward or outward, the outward hath beene handled in the former preface of this discourse, for unfolding the other wee must take in our way that maxime of philosophy, Simile simili gaudet or like will to like; . . . this is the cause why the Lord loves the Creature, soe farre as it hath any of his Image in it, he loves his elect because they are like himselfe, he beholds them in his beloved sonne: soe a mother loves her childe, because shee throughly conceives a resemblance of herselfe in it. Thus it is betweene the members of Christ, each discernes by the worke of the spirit his owne Image and resemblance in another, and therefore cannot but love him as he loves himselfe: Now when the soule which is of a sociable nature findes any thing like to it selfe, it is like Adam when Eve was brought to him, shee must have it one with herselfe this is fleshe of my fleshe (saith shee) and bone of my bone shee conceives a greate delighte in it, therefore shee desires nearnes and familiarity with it: shee hath a greate propensity to doe it good and receives such content in it, as feareing the miscarriage of her beloved shee bestowes it in the inmost closett of her heart, shee will not endure that it shall want any good which shee can give it, if by occasion shee be withdrawne from the Company of it, shee is still lookeing towards the place where shee left her beloved, if shee heare it groane shee is with it presently, if shee finde it sadd and disconsolate shee sighes and mournes with it, shee hath noe such joy, as to see her beloved merry and thriveing, if shee see it wronged, shee cannot beare it without passion, shee setts noe boundes of her affeccions, nor hath any thought of reward, shee findes recompence enoughe in the exercise of her love towardes it, wee may see this Acted to life in Jonathan and David. Jonathan a valiant man endued with the spirit of Christ, soe soone as hee Discovrs the same spirit in David had presently his hearte knitt to him by this linement of love, soe that it is said he loved him as his owne soule. . . . other instances might be brought to shewe the nature of this affeccion as of Ruthe and Naomi and many others, but this truthe is cleared enough. If any shall object that it is not possible that love should be bred or upheld without hope of requitall, it is graunted but that is not our cause, for this love is allwayes under reward it never gives, but it allwayes receives with advantage: first, in regard that among the members of the same body, love and affection are reciprocall in a most equall and sweete kinde of Commerce. 21y, in regard of the pleasure and content that the exercise of love carries with it as wee may see in the naturall body the mouth is at all the paines to receive, and mince the foode which serves for the nourishment of all the other partes of the body, yet it hath noe cause to complaine; for first, the other partes send backe by secret passages a due proporcion of the same nourishment in a better forme for the strengthening and comforteing the mouthe. 21y the labour of the mouthe is accompanied with such pleasure and content as farre exceedes the paines it takes: soe is it in all the labour of love, among christians, the partie loveing, reapes love againe as was shewed before, which the soule covetts more then all the wealthe in the world. . . . noething yeildes more pleasure and content to the soule then when it findes that which it may love fervently, for to love and live beloved is the soules paradice, both heare and in heaven: In the State of Wedlock there be many comfortes to beare out the troubles of that Condicion; but let such as have tryed the most, say if there be any sweetnes in that Condicion comparable to the exercise of mutuall love.

From the former Consideracions ariseth these Conclusions.

I First, This love among Christians is a reall thing not Imaginarie.

21y. This love is as absolutely necessary to the being of the body of Christ, as the sinewes and other ligaments of a naturall body are to the being of that body.

31y. This love is a divine spirituall nature free, active strong Couragious permanent under valueing all things beneathe its propper object, and of all the graces this makes us nearer to resemble the virtues of our heavenly father.

41y, It restes in the love and wellfare of its beloved, for the full and certaine knowledge of these truthes concerning the nature use, [and] excellency of this grace, that which the holy ghost hath left recorded I. Cor.

13. may give full satisfaccion which is needfull for every true member of this lovely body of the Lord Jesus, to worke upon theire heartes, by prayer meditacion continuall exercise at least of the speciall [power] of this grace till Christ be formed in them and they in him all in eache other knitt together by this bond of love.

It rests now to make some applicacion of this discourse by the present designe which gave the occasion of writeing of it. Herein are 4 things to be propounded: first the persons, 21y the worke, 31y the end, 41y the meanes.

I. For the persons, wee are a Company professing our selves fellow members of Christ, In which respect onely though wee were absent from eache other many miles, and had our imploymentes as farre distant, yet wee ought to account our selves knitt together by this bond of love, and live in the exercise of it, if wee would have comforte of our being in Christ, this was notorious in the practise of the Christians in former times, as is testified of the Waldenses from the mouth of one of the adversaries Aeneas Sylvius, mutuo [solent amare] pene antequam norint, they use to love any of theire owne religion even before they were acquainted with them.

21y. for the worke wee have in hand, it is by a mutuall consent through a speciall overruleing providence, and a more then an ordinary approbation of the Churches of Christ to seeke out a place of Cohabitation and Consorteshipp under a due forme of Goverment both civill and ecclesiasticall. In such cases as this the care of the publique must oversway all private respects, by which not onely conscience, but meare Civill pollicy doth binde us; for it is a true rule that perticuler estates cannott subsist in the ruine of the publique.

31y. The end is to improve our lives to doe more service to the Lord the comforte and encrease of the body of christe whereof wee are members that our selves and posterity may be the better preserved from the Common corrupcions of this evill world to serve the Lord and worke out our Salvacion under the power and purity of his holy Ordinances.

41y for the meanes whereby this must bee effected, they are 2fold, a Conformity with the worke and end wee aime at, these wee see are extraordinary, therefore wee must not content our selves with usuall ordinary meanes whatsoever wee did or ought to have done when wee lived in England, the same must wee doe and more allsoe where wee goe: That which the most in theire Churches maineteine as a truthe in profession onely, wee must bring into familiar and constant practise, as in this duty of love wee must love brotherly without dissimulation, wee must love one another with a pure hearte fervently wee must beare one anothers burthens, wee must not looke onely on our owne things, but allsoe on the things of our brethren, neither must wee think that the lord will beare with such faileings at our hands as hee dothe from those among whome wee have lived, and that for 3 Reasons.

I. In regard of the more neare bond of mariage, betweene him and us, wherein he hath taken us to be his after a most strickt and peculiar manner which will make him the more Jealous of our love and obedience soe he tells the people of Israell, you onely have I knowne of all the families of the Earthe therefore will I punishe you for your Transgressions.

21y, because the lord will be sanctified in them that come neare him. Wee know that there were many that corrupted the service of the Lord some setting upp Alters before his owne, others offering both strange fire and strange Sacrifices allsoe; yet there came noe fire from heaven, or other sudden Judgement upon them as did upon Nadab and Abihu whoe yet wee may thinke did not sinne presumptuously.

31y When God gives a speciall Commission he lookes to have it strictly observed in every Article, when hee gave Saule a Commission to destroy Amaleck hee indented with him upon certaine Articles and because hee failed in one of the least, and that upon a faire pretence, it lost him the kingdome, which should have beene his reward, if hee had observed his Commission: Thus stands the cause betweene God and us, wee are entered into Covenant with him for this worke, wee have taken out a Commission, the Lord hath given us leave to drawe our owne Articles wee have professed to enterprise these Accions upon these and these ends, wee have hereupon besought him of favour and blessing: Now if the Lord shall please to heare us, and bring us in peace to the place wee desire, then hath hee ratified this Covenant and sealed our Commission, [and] will expect a strickt performance of the Articles contained in it, but if wee shall neglect the observacion of these Articles which are the ends wee have propounded, and dissembling with our God, shall fall to embrace this present world and prosecute our carnall intencions, seekeing greate things for our selves and our posterity, the Lord will surely breake out in wrathe against us be revenged of such a perjured people and make us knowe the price of the breache of such a Covenant.

Now the onely way to avoyde this shipwracke and to provide for our posterity is to followe the Counsell of Micah, to doe Justly, to love mercy, to walke humbly with our God, for this end, wee must be knitt together in this worke as one man, wee must entertaine each other in brotherly Affeccion, wee must be willing to abridge our selves of our superfluities, for the supply of others necessities, wee must uphold a familiar Commerce together in all meekenes, gentlenes, patience and liberallity, wee must delight in eache other, make others Condicions our owne rejoyce together, mourne together, labour, and suffer together, allwayes haveing before our eyes our Commission and Community in the worke, our Community as members of the same body, soe shall wee keepe the unitie of the spirit in the bond of peace, the Lord will be our God and delight to dwell among us, as his owne people and will commaund a blessing upon us in all our wayes, soe that wee shall see much more of his wisdome power goodnes and truthe then formerly wee have beene acquainted with, wee shall finde that the God of Israell is among us, when tenn of us shall be able to resist a thousand of our enemies, when hee shall make us a prayse and glory, that men shall say of succeeding plantacions: the lord make it like that of New England: for wee must Consider that wee shall be as a Citty upon a Hill, the eies of all people are uppon us; soe that if wee shall deale falsely with our god in this worke wee have undertaken and soe cause him to withdrawe his present help from us, wee shall be made a story and a by-word through the world, wee shall open the mouthes of enemies to speake evill of the wayes of god and all professours for Gods sake; wee shall shame the faces of many of gods worthy servants, and cause theire prayers to be turned into Cursses upon us till wee be consumed out of the good land whether wee are goeing: And to shutt upp this discourse with that exhortacion of Moses that faithfull servant of the Lord in his last farewell to Israell Deut. 30. Beloved there is now sett before us life, and good, deathe and evill in that wee are Commaunded this day to love the Lord our God, and to love one another to walke in his wayes and to keepe his Commaundements and his Ordinance, and his lawes, and the Articles of our Covenant with him that wee may live and be multiplyed, and that the Lord our God may blesse us in the land whether wee goe to possesse it: But if our heartes shall turne away soe that wee will not obey, but shall be seduced and worshipp other Gods our pleasures, and proffitts, and serve them; it is propounded unto us this day, wee shall surely perishe out of the good Land whether wee passe over this vast Sea to possesse it;

Therefore lett us choose life,
that wee, and our Seede,
may live; by obeyeing his
voyce, and cleaveing to him,
for hee is our life, and
our prosperity.

Part three ══════

══════ Bibliographic Essay

Historians have seldom considered Winthrop's personal decision for America apart from the larger question of the motivation for the 1630 migration to New England. Thus, insofar as Winthrop was part of the mass of "Puritan" settlers, his emigration has been variously interpreted as divinely inspired (this by such seventeenth century historians as Edward Johnson in his *A History of New-England From the English planting in the Yeere 1628, untill the Yeere 1652* [London, 1654]); as the result of religious persecution (Cotton Mather, *Magnalia Christı Americana; or, The Ecclesiastical History of New-England* [London, 1702]); as a flight of liberty-loving Englishmen from Stuart tyranny (the "Whig" interpretation rising in the late eighteenth century, prevalent through most of the nineteenth, and well exemplified by John Adams, "A Dissertation on the Canon and Feudal Law," in *The Works of John Adams,* ed. Charles Francis Adams, vol. III [Boston, 1851]); as inspired by economic difficulties in England and economic opportunities in America (James Truslow Adams, *The Founding of New England* [Boston, 1921]); and as a conscious attempt to put into practice a particular and peculiar doctrine of church polity of "non-separating congregationalism" (Perry Miller, *Orthodoxy in Massachusetts, 1630-1650* [Cambridge, Mass., 1930]). Winthrop's first major biographer, Robert C. Winthrop, in his *Life and Letters of John Winthrop,* 2 vols. (Boston, 1863-66) contented himself with simply printing Winthrop's rationalization of his decision, notably Documents 7 and 8, letting this suffice to display motivation. Edmund S. Morgan, in a remarkable modern interpretation (*The Puritan Dilemma: The Story of John Winthrop* [Boston, 1958]), placed Winthrop's decision in the context of the Puritan mind as sketched by Miller, particularly in Miller's *The New England Mind: The Seventeenth Century* (Boston, 1939). Samuel Eliot Morison in 1930 ("John Winthrop, Esquire" in his *Builders of the Bay Colony* [Boston and New York]) and Carl Bridenbaugh in 1968 (*Vexed and Troubled Englishmen, 1590-1642* [New York]) saw Winthrop as responding to a very broad English situation, one involving a feeling of social, political, and economic, as well as religious discomfort. Bridenbaugh, too, although in a general context and not specifically with regard to Winthrop, added the sociological notion of emigration as a response to both "pushes" (negative factors making one uncomfortable in the old country) and "pulls" (positive images of the possible resolution of difficulties in the new). An interpretation of Winthrop responding to a broad spectrum of vexations leads one axiomatically to English history of the period and particularly to the works of Lawrence Stone (*The Crisis of the Aristocracy, 1558-1641* [Oxford, 1965], *The Causes of the English Revolution: 1529-1642* [London, 1972]) and Perez Zagorin (*The Court & the Country: The Beginning of the English Revolution* [London, 1968]) who have well developed the notion of the "Country mind." It also leads one to a theoretical consideration of motivation and decision making, and just how far the historian can go in bridging the gap between the general (vexed Englishmen) and the particular (Winthrop's decision) on the basis of the remnants of the past (in this case, the documents). In this regard, Robert F. Berkhofer, Jr.'s *A Behavioral Approach to Historical Analysis* (New York, 1969) can do much to bring Winthrop's decision into focus.